Legacy of Impact

The Determined Path to Success, True Leadership, and Giving Back

Tolulope Michael

Contents

INTRODUCTION

We live in a new world that demands more from us than ever. People no longer want an ordinary job but one with true fulfillment. Think about your place in life right now. Are you at a point where you are tired of working tirelessly just to get by? Or are you searching for a new career to create the kind of life you want? Maybe you want one with flexibility and an opportunity to make a real difference. You might have tried breaking into a high-paying industry like tech and given up because of the long path of education, training, and certification.

If all of these sound familiar, believe me when I know exactly where you're coming from. Because I have been in your shoes, I know where it hurts.

Like you, I was once at this crossroads. That's right. There was a time when I worked menial jobs and did whatever was necessary to make ends meet. Despite my efforts, this wasn't enough to keep me afloat. I was physically drained, mentally exhausted, and stuck. I yearned for something more. I dreamed about having a career that could pay my worth and let me live on my terms. But then, I wasn't sure how to make that happen.

That all changed when I stumbled upon cybersecurity by pure luck and fate. Today, I am a leading authority in an industry with endless opportunities, earning six figures. Don't think I'm saying this to impress you; I aim to show you that anyone, including you, can be in my current position. Yes, you can make the transition, no matter your current background.

Right about now, you're probably wondering, "HOW?"

When most people consider a career change, they see a path lined with barriers—prerequisites they believe they don't meet. Advanced degrees, specialized skills, years of experience. The stories they tell themselves begin with "I'm not qualified" and end with a resignation to staying stuck. For years, I thought the same. I assumed success in a new field was reserved for those with the perfect credentials or insider access to opportunities.

That belief was wrong.

Success in a new career isn't defined by what you don't have—it's shaped by what you're willing to do. It doesn't require a flawless resume or a predefined trajectory. It demands clarity, the courage to start, and a commitment to follow a proven system.

I know this because I've lived it. I transitioned from jobs that barely paid the bills to a career that opened doors I once thought were locked forever. I didn't have the "perfect" background. I didn't have unlimited resources. But I had a clear plan, the discipline to execute it, and the mindset to keep going even when it felt like the odds were against me.

This isn't just about my story—it's about yours. It's about the potential you already possess, waiting to be unlocked. It's about the opportunities hiding in plain sight, just waiting for you to claim them. You don't need to have all the answers right now. You only need to be willing to learn, take action, and trust that success is possible, even when the path isn't obvious.

The truth is, the tools to achieve your goals are closer than you think, and this book is your guide to doing just that. It's not about overwhelming you with theories or concepts. It's about showing you how to make real, actionable progress—how to move from where you are to where you want to be. Whether you're contemplating a career pivot, aiming for professional growth, or simply seeking a path that aligns with your values, the strategies here will give you the direction you need.

If you're ready to invest in yourself, challenge your assumptions, and create something extraordinary, this book is for you. If you're looking for someone to tell you it's okay to stay where you are, you won't find that here. Change requires action, and action requires commitment.

The question isn't whether change is possible. The question is whether you're ready to take the first step. This journey is about transformation, and that transformation came through cybersecurity. It's a field that changed my life and has the power to do the same for countless others. So, why cybersecurity? I'll tell you.

"Why Cybersecurity?"

It's okay if this question is raging loudly in your head. After all, why should you choose this particular field over all others? The answer is straightforward: cybersecurity is one of the fastest-growing fields in the world right now, and if stats mean anything, it'll continue for decades. Despite the global economic challenges, the demand for cybersecurity professionals continues to surge without one sign of decline in sight.

Around the world, companies and governments are facing increasing threats to their digital systems. Consequently, they need skilled individuals to protect their networks, data, and assets. Currently, there are millions of unfulfilled cybersecurity jobs globally. In fact, North America alone has more than 900,000 open positions in cybersecurity. Someone like you needs to step in and fill these roles.

What does this mean for you?

It means that you have an opportunity right here, right now. This field offers job security, high income, and, more importantly, the potential to work from the comfort of your home, no matter where you are. Flexibility is assured whether you'd prefer to work remotely, like I do, or become part of a team in an office environment. Perhaps the cherry on top is that you can do meaningful work. You get to protect businesses, organizations, and even governments from cyber threats.

The best part? You don't need years of schooling or a background in IT to get started. You need the right roadmap, and that's what this book is about.

If you're still wondering why cybersecurity, I'll tell you why.

The truth is, we're in a critical moment right now. Companies of all sizes, from startups to Fortune 500 corporations, face unprecedented challenges in securing digital assets. Data breaches, ransomware attacks, and cyber threats are rising, and businesses are scrambling to protect themselves. Unfortunately, there are financial costs for every company vulnerable to a cyberattack.

Beyond that lies trust. Vulnerability can make clients lose confidence, customers feel unsafe, and businesses fall apart. That is why cybersecurity is highly sought after today, and it's where you come in.

The good news is that companies aren't looking for experts to fill the millions of unoccupied roles. They value soft skills—critical thinking, problem-solving, and adaptability—just as much, if not more, than technical experience.

Why This Book is Different

The world is brimming with advice about achieving success, yet much of it feels inaccessible. You're told to collect degrees, certifications, and years of experience before daring to chase your goals. This kind of guidance often reinforces the doubts and fears that keep people stuck. It paints success as reserved for others—those with resources, connections, or the "right" background.

This book defies that narrative. It's not just about strategies or principles—it reflects my journey and is a practical guide rooted in real-life experiences. It's proof that success isn't about fitting into a mold but about learning how to move forward with purpose and intention, regardless of where you start.

This book is unique because it focuses on personal growth and lasting impact. It's not only about advancing your career or achieving financial security, though those are certainly important. It's about building a life that matters—one that aligns with your values and leaves a mark on the world. Success isn't just about what you gain but about what you create and contribute along the way.

Every insight shared here comes from lived experience—my own and those I've guided through career transformations. This is not an abstract theory or distant observation. I've faced the same struggles many of you are navigating right now, and I've helped others overcome similar challenges. Their stories remind you that change is not just possible—it's attainable.

This book doesn't offer cookie-cutter solutions or overcomplicated jargon. Instead, it gives you tools to reimagine your potential and take steps tailored to your unique situation. You'll learn to identify opportunities, overcome obstacles, and chart a course that aligns with your strengths and ambitions.

What sets this book apart is its personal connection. It's not about impersonal advice or generic formulas. It's about sharing the real-life journeys of people who dared to challenge their circumstances and found ways to create a future they once thought was out of reach. Their experiences are a testament to the power of action, persistence, and belief in the possibility of something better.

This isn't just a book to read; it's an invitation to act. It's for those ready to challenge the limits placed on them and embrace the process of building something meaningful. It's for those who want more than fleeting success; they want impact.

This book may reflect my journey, but it's also an offering for yours. You won't just be chasing goals; you will be redefining what's possible and creating a future that inspires you and those around you.

I will show you how to:

- Identify the industries and high-demand roles and align

them with your unique skills and strengths.

- Leverage your existing experience to create a compelling professional narrative, even if it feels unrelated to your goals.
- Position yourself as the ideal candidate for opportunities in your chosen field, even if you lack traditional qualifications or prior experience.
- Accelerate your path to success with clear, practical steps to begin implementing today.

By the end of this book, you will have a clear roadmap for accelerating your career in ways you didn't think possible until now. You'll have the confidence, knowledge, and tools you need to succeed, and most importantly, you'll believe that you can do this—because you can.

Let's break down what you can expect from *Legacy of Impact* further.

As I said, we aren't doing theory in this book. I am providing you with fundamental tools and practical steps that you can implement immediately to make your dream happen.

Here's what you can expect to learn:

- **Understanding the cybersecurity landscape.** You'll gain a clearer understanding of cybersecurity beyond the misconceptions and jargon. I'll show you the different roles within this field that don't require being a tech expert. Even better, I will tell you all about the domains of cybersecurity, including governance, risk, and compliance, and how the skills you have now can fit into them.

- **Identifying the right path for you.** Cybersecurity isn't a one-size-fits-all career. Whether you have a background in customer service, administration, project management, or education, you have a role in cybersecurity. We'll explore the different areas where soft skills like communication, problem-solving, and attention to detail are just as critical as technical expertise. You'll learn to assess your current skills and identify the cybersecurity roles that best suit your strengths.

- **Leveraging certifications without breaking the bank.** While many believe certifications are the only way to get into cybersecurity, this isn't always true. Certifications can be helpful, but they don't need to cost you thousands of dollars. In this book, I'll show you how to prioritize the certifications that matter most for the specific role you're aiming for. We'll also cover affordable options for gaining the necessary certifications without spending a fortune on boot camps or courses that don't deliver results.

- **Accelerating your career once you're in.** Breaking into cybersecurity is just the beginning. Once you land your first job, there are countless opportunities for growth and advancement. This book will show you how to continue learning, upskilling, and positioning yourself for promotions and higher-paying roles. You'll learn how to build a career that pays well and offers job security and personal satisfaction.

Taking the First Step

The biggest mistake people make is waiting too long to start. They tell themselves they're not ready, need more experience, or don't have the right background. But the truth is, you'll never feel 100% ready. The key is to take action anyway. This book is designed to give you the confidence and the tools to start your journey today, no matter where you're starting from.

You don't need to have all the answers right now. That's why I have written this to guide you through each step of the process, from understanding the industry to landing your first six-figure job. If you're willing to follow the steps outlined here, you'll be surprised at how quickly things can change.

The path to success and impact is not as complex as you might think. It's accessible, rewarding, and, most importantly, achievable for anyone willing to do the work. As long as you read this book to the very end, you'll have a clear plan of action and the confidence to pursue a career in one of the world's most exciting and in-demand industries.

Taking this determined path to success isn't just about acquiring new skills. Your very first step must be to adopt a new mindset. You don't want to be one of those who hold themselves back due to limiting beliefs like, *"Oh, but I'm not qualified enough"* or *"I don't think I have the right background to succeed in this field."* Trust me, I almost let this happen, too. But I realized later that my mindset nearly held me back, not my lack of experience. The belief that you need the perfect resume or years of training is a trap designed to keep you in the same spot for as long as possible. The fact is that you're more ready than you think.

That's why a mindset shift is pivotal at this juncture. You need it to move from where you are now to where you want to be. I'm not saying you must be the most intelligent person in the room or prepare all your answers upfront. But you need a willingness to learn, persistence, and an openness to new opportunities. Tell yourself that you belong in the cybersecurity space and that your skills—no matter what—will be valuable.

To succeed in this field, you must embrace a growth mindset. By this, I mean understanding that failure is part of this journey. You won't know everything when you start, and that's okay. What matters is your ability to keep pushing forward, learning, and using every setback as a rung to success.

This book teaches you how to approach cybersecurity with a growth mindset. I'll show you how to position yourself for success, even if you come from an entirely different field. Remember that you don't need to be a tech wizard to thrive in this space. You only need the belief that you can learn, grow, and make a real impact.

You've read this far, so you're serious about improving your life. You are ready to leave limitations behind and embrace a financially secure future, just as I once did. But you must never forget that reading alone won't make the change you desire; your actions will.

None of this book's information, insights, and practical steps will matter without you doing what it takes. There's an opportunity right in front of you that you must reach out and grab immediately. Do not wait for the perfect time because it'll never come. Do not wait until you feel a hundred percent ready because you will never be. The only way to succeed is to start before you're ready, learn as you go, and adapt. I am offering you the opportunity to do that with this book.

It's time to take the proverbial first step. But for now, all you need to focus on is taking that first step. The journey ahead will have challenges, but it will also be gratifying. You'll learn, grow, and build a career that you can be proud of. Most importantly, you'll create a legacy of impact with a job that changes your life and makes a real difference.

Your journey to success starts now. Let's begin.

In the next chapter, I will take you deeper into my journey. You'll see firsthand how I went from working minimum-wage jobs and struggling to get by to breaking into cybersecurity and earning six figures in a matter of months. It wasn't an easy path and didn't happen overnight, but it's proof that anything is possible with the right mindset and a step-by-step plan.

By sharing my story, I hope to show you that your breakthrough is closer than you think, no matter where you start. So, let's get started with humble beginnings—where my journey began.

From Humble Beginnings: My Journey to Six Figures

How an African immigrant's journey started with menial jobs and a vision for a better future. The foundation of success begins here.

Usually, when people hear the word "immigrant," they think of someone from an impoverished country coming to the First World for better opportunities and an improved quality of life. This is true to an extent, but most African immigrants were doing relatively well back home before deciding to move abroad. Such was my case.

Before moving to the U.S., I had a steady life as an administrative officer in the Lagos State government. Though this role wasn't the peak of what I envisioned, the job assured my financial security. I could afford to eat what I wanted, live where I wanted, and live the unattainable life for many in Nigeria. Plus, I had friends, family, and routines, which resulted in a sense of familiarity. I found that comforting.

At the same time, I constantly thought about my future—my dreams, goals, aspirations, and ambitions. They were bigger than what Nigeria had to offer. But was I willing to leap and pursue the opportunities out there? It took me a while to answer this question confidently, but I was indeed willing. So, I started preparing to leave my homeland.

I knew I wanted more from life. As long as I remained in Nigeria, there would always be a ceiling, no matter how hard I worked. I could be the most qualified and ambitious person, and opportunities would still be limited. I'm not saying Nigeria has no potential; it does. Unfortunately, it has less to do with what a person is capable of and more with who they know. This is the reality.

When an opportunity came around to move to the U.S., I jumped at it and grabbed it by the horns. Eagerly, I packed my bags and said goodbye to everything I knew. The excitement was electrifying, but so was the apprehension. In my mind, I could picture myself working hard, climbing up the ladder, and becoming the person I had always wanted to be—the American dream. But reality took no time to sink in.

I arrived in the U.S. full of hope but soon realized I would have difficulty breaking into corporate America. The fact that I came from a respectable position in Nigeria didn't seem to matter much, nor did my experience. I tried my best, but the doors to corporate jobs remained closed. In this land of dreams, I was just another immigrant, another face in the crowd, here to begin my life's journey from scratch.

To support myself and stay afloat, I took on every minimum-wage job I could find. These jobs were starkly in contrast to my previous professional experience. I had never worked any job like that before I moved to the U.S. But what choice did I have? Putting food on the table was imperative.

So, I started working as a delivery rider for Uber, Amazon, and Doordash, you name it. I even worked in factories and warehouses, which were considered the lowest of the lows for immigrants. The experience was humbling, to say the least. Still, I persevered because I knew this was all a process. I only had to prove myself, and something better would come my way.

The Struggle

I am being a hundred percent candid when I say that starting from the very bottom in a new country was beyond challenging. It humbled me in ways that shook my very core. And why wouldn't it? I had come from a job with a desk, a title, and a sense of purpose, and I was secure in the ways that matter. Yet, once I arrived in the U.S., I felt stripped of my purpose and security. My new reality meant earning my place in an unfamiliar society from the ground up. It wasn't glamorous, and this part of the story isn't what most people like to hear, but it was the reality for me then.

As I mentioned, I started taking on delivery gigs, which I would never have pictured myself doing in a million years. The first few weeks were rough for me. Getting used to the ins and outs of the delivery world—finding the right location and managing traffic—took some time. But I persevered to keep a roof over my head and food on the table.

Each day was a cycle of logging into different apps, driving across town, and delivering people's packages to their doorsteps. Some days, I stayed on the road for hours, usually well into the night. I'd watch people going about their lives, friends laughing together, or families gathering around the table as I delivered their dinner. I'd start to miss my loved ones in Nigeria so profoundly. I also felt a pang of envy sometimes because these people were living the kind of life I desired, while my only choice was to hustle hard to get by.

The factory and warehouse jobs were particularly demanding, both physically and mentally. Sometimes, I spent hours on my feet, lifting heavy loads and moving stock. In the factory, it was the same daily routine with never-ending noises. I wasn't used to this, but this was my surest way to earn a living until I found something better. Understandably, I couldn't afford to be picky.

Some moments stand out now—times when I questioned my decision to come to America. I remember a specific day after an incredibly exhausting shift. I found a corner and sat down like the world's weight was on my shoulders. I looked at the blisters that had formed from handling boxes all day. I felt the ache in my back and the soreness in my muscles. At that moment, I burst into tears and asked myself, *Is this really worth it*? I wondered if I had made a mistake coming to the United States. But even at that moment, I refused to give up my dream. I had come too far. And deep down, I knew I was where I was supposed to be.

I learned something new from every gig I worked. Being a delivery rider meant I needed to master patience and hone an eye for details. Meanwhile, working in factories required stamina and focus. Consequently, I had to adapt and find my rhythm for whatever job I was working. This taught me to push through regardless of how tired I may feel. It also taught me to find pride in whatever I did for money, even if such a job differed significantly from my dreams.

Each day, I reminded myself that every successful person started from somewhere, and this was my own genesis. I stood in front of a mirror and reminded myself of my purpose. I reminded myself that these menial jobs were stepping stones to something bigger. My vision remained clear as a bright, sunny day—I was in America to do more than survive. I had to build something to establish a future that would make my struggles and sacrifices worth it.

Working minimum-wage jobs renewed my perspective about the hard work and sacrifice that went into getting certain things done. I realized I wasn't above any job or too proud to do whatever it took. While challenging, my early experiences as an immigrant shaped me and made me more resilient than ever. They transformed me into the person I am today.

In the past, I was one of those who looked at successful people and assumed they'd always had things easy. I now know that is rarely the case. To succeed in life, one must be willing to pave the road with sweat and sacrifice. It's about doing the things no one else dares to do, facing the struggles no one else sees, and staying strong when you're so close to breaking down and giving everything up.

Finding Faith and Community

Despite my struggles and challenges, there was one constant I could always count on—my faith. It was my anchor, the one thing that kept me sane. Back at home, I gave my life to Christ in 2007 and have remained a faithful Christian ever since. My dedication to my faith has shaped me in different ways, even in ways I am still discovering. Regardless of how tough my situation got, I was confident that God had a purpose for me. He guided me toward the right path, even though I couldn't see it, and many thought I was merely wandering aimlessly. My faith in God and religion kept me grounded, especially on days when I felt isolated and alone.

On a fateful Sunday Morning, I headed to church as always. The previous week had been particularly tough, thanks to various long shifts and very little sleep. I found myself feeling utterly drained. I must have looked as worn out as I felt because, after the service, one of the brothers at church approached me. He must have seen right through me because he asked, "What's going on? Are you okay?" At first, I tried to brush it off with the usual, "I'm okay," but he wasn't buying it. He looked me in the eye and said, "No, really. What's going on with you?"

In that moment, everything I had been holding in came pouring out. I told this brother-in-Christ about my struggle—the jobs I was working, the stress, and the frustration of feeling stuck no matter how hard I worked. I didn't expect anything; I was just glad to have someone willing to listen to me express my pain, fears, and frustrations. He listened patiently, without judgment, and then when I had finished, he calmly said that single statement that changed the trajectory of my life: "Why not give cybersecurity a try?"

I was taken aback. It wasn't that I was hearing about cybersecurity before—I was familiar with the term and field. But I'd be lying if I said I had ever considered it as a career path before that day. When I thought about it then, I pictured hackers and complex codes. That was far too technical for my skill set. It was out of my league, so to speak. I told him as much, but he smiled and reassured me. "It's not as complicated as you think," he said. "And you'd be surprised at the demand in the field. I think you'd be great at it."

He further explained that he had helped others through the transition, people from different backgrounds. He assured me again that I could do it and he would guide me through the process.

For the first time in an excruciatingly long time, I felt a surge of hope awaken within me. I remember feeling excited, curious, and doubtful. My emotions were firing on all fronts. It was as though someone had opened a door I didn't even know existed.

I started asking all kinds of questions—how would I begin? What would I need? Blah, blah, blah. He was very helpful in walking me through the steps, the courses I would have to take, what certifications to get, what skills to learn, etc. He put me through pretty much everything with patience and encouragement and without any hesitation.

From that moment on, I decided to give cybersecurity a shot. This was my chance to *really* rebuild and take charge of my future as I have always dreamed I could. I had a new direction and a renewed sense of purpose. I didn't have to feel stuck ever again. And in that moment, I knew my faith had led me here.

When I think of that Sunday, I view it as nothing short of a divine intervention. Perhaps I wouldn't be where I am today if I hadn't gone to church on that day if I hadn't opened up about my struggles. And so, I credit God, my church community, and that brother who took the time to talk to me. I believe that God put that brother in my path for a reason. It was a reminder that even in the darkest times, there's guidance if you're willing to see it.

This experience taught me something invaluable about community, too. Moving to a new country can be incredibly isolating. You're away from your family, your friends, everything familiar. But finding a church gave me a sense of belonging. It connected me with people who cared and could lift me up when I struggled. It reminded me that we're not meant to do this alone.

I've carried that lesson with me ever since. No matter where you are in life, never underestimate the power of community. Surround yourself with people who believe in you and push you to see beyond your current situation. Sometimes, all it takes is one conversation to change the course of your life.

Discovering Cybersecurity

Contrary to your opinion, my decision to pursue cybersecurity didn't instantly change my life. As a matter of fact, the process brought with it a fresh set of challenges. The difference was that I had a goal now—I was no longer working for survival. I was working to make something tangible of my migration. There was a clear path before me that I was determined to see through. I'll tell you for free that nothing is more motivating in life than having a clear goal and a step-by-step guide to achieve that goal. As my people would say, I was really *gingered.*

The first thing I did as soon as I got home from church that Sunday was to research. I wanted to know as much as possible about cybersecurity, the skills I needed, etc. I dived into every piece of information I could find on Google, blogs, and forums and tried my best to collate it all. Naturally, I was overwhelmed by the vast amount of information available online. I encountered terms like "threat analysis, "network security," and "penetration testing" for the first time, and they were baffling—like a foreign language. But I wrote everything down in a notebook and watched many YouTube videos for a breakdown. This allowed me to assimilate the information better.

After a few days of research, I decided I would need formal training to start my cybersecurity journey. So, I found an introductory course online and enrolled. This self-paced program gave me enough time to juggle my other jobs with learning successfully. I dedicated my evenings to studying, sometimes late into the night. This was exhausting, but the feeling of accomplishment I felt every time I completed a module or passed a test was exhilarating.

In this introductory course, I learned about the basics of cybersecurity, from the different types of cyber threats to firewalls and encryption. I could tell there was so much more to know as I went from module to module. It wasn't easy–learning alone meant feeling frustrated whenever I had trouble grasping a concept or hit another kind of roadblock. I was also eager to make myself skilled enough for a well-paying job. Whenever I felt frustrated, I would remind myself of where I began and where I wanted to be. Visualizing the life I wanted always helped to bring me back on track.

Eventually, I started preparing to get the necessary certifications. This was one of my major milestones. The brother from church had told me to get a few, like CompTIA Security+, Certified Ethical Hacker, and, subsequently, CISSP. I needed these certifications to establish myself as a skilled talent in the cybersecurity field. I had to save up to get them because the exam wasn't cheap. It was a critical investment, my ticket to the much-anticipated future.

In and of itself, studying for the CompTIA+ exam was an experience. I spent hours reviewing practice questions, tutorials, reading exam guides—anything useful. My study material was dense, and I sometimes wondered if I could pull it off. Still, I'd remind myself occasionally that even the experts were once beginners. One thing that made it easier was setting small goals daily, which significantly boosted my progress.

I will never forget the feeling I had on the exam day. This was *make* or *break*. I still visibly remember myself in front of the computer, taking a deep breath and asking God to join me in starting and finishing the exam. The good thing is I was fully prepared for the tough questions. At the end, when I answered the final question and clicked on "Submit," I felt a wave of profound relief. My results came out a few days later; I'd passed. Believe me, that was the turning point. It was proof that I could do this. I had faced and overcame the first hurdle, and the feeling was incredible.

When I passed that exam, I got more than a certification. I got validation—it was proof that putting in the work would pay off. I did more than just learn new skills; I changed my mindset. I went from being someone who did whatever he could to get by to someone with a purpose and a budding career. And that was more than enough fuel to keep me going.

I kept studying, taking more courses, and earning more certifications. Every additional course or certification felt like a piece of the puzzle falling into place. With the help of that brother from church, I began networking and reaching out to others in the field. They shared tips, ideas, and experiences that immensely benefited my growth. I also attended virtual meetups, joined online groups, and sought out mentors who could guide me.

Things weren't always smooth sailing. Some days, I felt overwhelmed by the sheer volume of information I needed to learn. Cybersecurity is a fast-evolving field, and keeping up with the latest trends and developments was challenging. But I embraced it, knowing that every challenge was an opportunity for growth.

Looking back, cybersecurity gave me direction when I felt lost, purpose when I needed it most, and a new identity as someone who could thrive in a challenging and rewarding field. It was the path I hadn't planned on but one I was grateful to have found.

The American Dream, Imagined

My new path made me start to see the U.S. in a new light. Hearing about the American dream from a continent away is one thing; living it is another. As I have explained before, opportunities in Africa (and Nigeria) are pretty limited. Hard work isn't enough. People need connections for good opportunities. Even then, a person's success might be capped by factors beyond their control.

The reality is different in America. In this country, I was free to reinvent myself without constraints. Despite where I came from and the jobs I had done in the past, I knew I could build a new life from scratch based on my skills and willingness to learn. As long as you're willing to put in the effort and make sacrifices, the U.S. presents opportunities to grow, advance, and achieve things you never thought possible.

One significant difference between Nigeria and the U.S. is the culture of meritocracy. Here, it's clear that putting effort into whatever you want will most likely pay off. In fact, the chances of failure are slim. You don't need connections or people in high places to find your footing and get ahead. You just need to put in the work. So, I was confident that if I could earn the proper certifications and gain the right skills, then doors would open for me. And they did.

Sure, my life in Nigeria was comfortable, but there was a ceiling to what I could aspire to or achieve. Living in the U.S. lifted this ceiling. I could dream bigger and aim higher. It didn't matter that I'd started as a delivery rider or spent months working minimum-wage jobs. What mattered was that I could keep moving forward and building.

"I was born in Nigeria but made in the U.S." People around me will tell you this is one of my favorite sayings ever. Why? Because it encapsulates my journey perfectly. Nigeria gave me my foundation—my values, faith, and resilience. But in the U.S., I found the opportunity to apply these qualities and use them to build something great. I've made a life here that would have been out of reach back home, and I am deeply grateful for that.

Now, I'm not saying that the U.S. is without challenges. Even now, there are moments when I feel like an outsider when the cultural differences and the weight of being far from home hit me hard. These moments only strengthen my resolve, though. Primarily to help other people of similar backgrounds who are having trouble establishing a worthwhile career overseas.

Thanks to the opportunities I found in this beautiful country, I can do things I never imagined. I have built a successful career in an exciting field. I earn an income that is more than enough to support myself and my loved ones back home. I am constantly contributing to something bigger than me. Most importantly, I am laying the foundation for a legacy that inspires others.

Every day, I remind myself that I am living proof of what's possible in this country. The United States of America may not be perfect, but it's the best place I could have rewritten my story. It's a place where hard work can lead to real success, where you can build something that lasts. And as someone who has come from a place where such opportunities are rare, I don't take any of this for granted.

For anyone reading this who might feel limited by their circumstances, I want you to know that change is possible. Yes, it won't be easy. Yes, it will require a lot of sacrifice, patience, and a willingness to start over. But if you're willing to put in the work, you can achieve things beyond what you ever thought possible. I've seen it firsthand, and I'm living proof that you can reimagine your American Dream with faith, hard work, and the right mindset.

Building My Legacy

Over the past year, I found myself introspecting more and more on what I wanted my journey to represent. I am proud of the milestones I have reached. Moving to a six-figure income from working factory jobs is no simple feat. But I want there to be more to my story than the financial gains. The struggles I faced on this path were more than mere obstacles. They were lessons, and I intend to use them to build a legacy of impact—one that will live on beyond my success.

In my belief, building a legacy entails creating a path that others can follow to success. God has blessed me with opportunities that transformed my life. As such, I feel responsible for helping people like you see that these opportunities exist for you, too. I remember what it is like to feel stuck and as though you're standing still as the world moves forward. If I can use my story to inspire others facing similar challenges, then all the struggles I went through were worth it.

I have started building my legacy by sharing my journey with others. Currently, I have spoken at various community events and shared my experiences with new immigrants and those considering a profitable career change.

Many people can relate to my struggles, including the challenge of starting over, the fear of failure, and the uncertainty of stepping into a new field. That's why I want to show you that you don't have to be defined by where you came from or what you've been through. If I can build a new life from scratch, so can you.

Building a life from scratch in a foreign country taught me humility, perseverance, and faith lessons. But the real test of my resolve came from barriers I could never have imagined—cultural, financial, and mental. These challenges shaped the next phase of my journey.

What happened next?

Behind every success story lies a series of obstacles that test your determination, and mine was no different. I didn't just wake up one day and find myself in a high-paying career. I overcame setbacks, doubts, and the reality of starting over in a completely unfamiliar environment.

In the next chapter, I'll explore those challenges further. You'll see the specific struggles I faced along the way, from adjusting to a new culture to battling financial stress to overcoming the mental hurdles that could have held me back. More importantly, I'll show you how I turned those obstacles into ladder rungs. The key to success isn't avoiding challenges; it's learning to overcome them.

Let's dive into the next step in my journey, where the real work began.

Challenging the Odds: How I overcame Obstacles Along the Way

The struggles and barriers immigrants face in foreign countries, and how perseverance can defy the odds.

The path to success is rarely smooth. Though reaching this point in my career has been a defining moment, the road I followed was far from easy. My journey required resilience, sacrifice, and an unshakeable determination to achieve personal and professional growth despite the odds being stacked against me.

We've explored how I began my career transformation together, but there's more to my story than that first step I took. When people talk about others' success stories, what often goes unspoken are the countless obstacles that threaten to derail one's progress.

Even though the brother from church had set me on a potentially rewarding path, I still faced quite several hurdles. From adjusting to a new culture to managing financial strain, every challenge I faced could have held me back. Instead, I turned each one into a learning and growth opportunity. I was desperate to prove that I was capable of more, and I did.

Here, I will tell you all about the odds I defied and the obstacles I overcame along the way. Those moments tested my strength and forced me to confront the limitations I once thought would define me. For me, the process wasn't just about navigating a new career. I was determined to push through the personal and professional barriers that stood in the way of real success.

Navigating an Unfamiliar World

Starting a new career in a field where you have little to no experience requires mastering an entirely new way of interacting and working. Although getting employed in a cybersecurity role meant I could work from anywhere, the transition still wasn't easy. Landing my first role took countless hours of preparation, plenty of trials and errors, and immense effort. The cultural differences were a different layer of complication that took time to adjust.

Once I had everything necessary for applying to cybersecurity jobs, my biggest challenge was standing out in the U.S. job market. Having the skills wasn't close to being enough. I had to learn to present myself in ways that resonated with American employers. Plus, corporate America was a brand new world that I didn't yet know how to navigate.

As such, crafting my resume, applying for relevant jobs, and networking remotely required excellent strategic thinking and positioning. Believe me when I say I spent hundreds of hours researching, fine-tuning my applications, and attending networking events—both online and in real life. I focused on building the right connections to get me where I wanted.

This process took much more time than I had anticipated. Every rejection shot a dart at my heart but also pushed me to work even harder. I invested time and money into advanced training and certifications to improve my qualifications so employers could no longer tell me no.

I knew that having technical knowledge and the right skills wouldn't do all the work for me. I had to show employers I could thrive in a remote work environment, communicate effectively across cultures, and fit into teams I had never met. Obviously, I couldn't achieve this with a one-time effort. I had to dedicate a substantial amount of time to refining my skills, improving my resume, and coming up with new ways to stand out in the job market.

As you might have guessed, the cultural aspects of remote work also posed significant challenges. Sure, communication happened primarily through screens. Nevertheless, nuances of communication were heavily shaped by the American workplace culture, whether we were communicating via virtual meetings, instant messages, or emails.

Getting used to these subtle differences took time. Sometimes, I worked twice as hard just to adapt. I was even unfamiliar with simple things, such as navigating casual conversations or presenting myself properly in virtual meetings. Still, I knew that adjusting to these differences would help me build vital professional relationships in my new career.

Sometimes, after yet another rejection, I felt like I wasn't making headway on this path. That made me toy with the idea of abandoning cybersecurity and focusing on the physical jobs that put food on my table. Then, I would shake out of the delusion and remind myself that God set me on this road for a reason.

At the same time, the isolation of working remotely was challenging. It made me feel disconnected from the rest of the world. This is something only people who have tried breaking into a new sector from the outside would relate to. Still, I persevered and held on to the belief that everything would pay off eventually. Persistence was my mantra in those days.

Ultimately, all that hard work, a growth mindset, and an adaptable attitude landed me my first cybersecurity job. Throughout this process, I learned that success is unattainable without a willingness to learn, adapt, and push through setbacks.

What's my point?

To break into cybersecurity, especially in a remote role, you'll need more than the skills or knowledge you acquire in this book or your training. You'll need hard work, persistence, and a readiness to master your new environment's cultural and professional nuances. Don't forget that only those who keep pushing even in the face of uncertainty will succeed.

Financial Struggles: Surviving the Tough Early Days

Anyone who has ever had to start over will tell you that the financial reality check that comes with it demands urgency. When I began my transition, I still had to find ways to maintain financial stability. For this, I needed to do more than earn; I needed to be creative in stretching every dollar as I pursued my long-term goals. This meant that I had to constantly rethink every purchase, every expense, and every financial decision to keep myself on track toward my desired future.

Understandably, it would be impossible to achieve my goals without great financial discipline. So, I steeled myself and made some very tough decisions regarding spending. This was necessary to carve out a path forward. As soon as I received my paycheck, I would first focus on the essentials: housing, food, and the basic stuff I needed for support. I couldn't afford luxuries and unnecessary expenses at that stage. Being strict and setting limits on spending was non-negotiable, and I habitually reviewed my budget every other week to ensure I was on track.

One strategy that made a remarkable difference in my finances was doing a comprehensive breakdown of my expenses. There was zero room for guesswork, which meant using spreadsheets and notes to track where every dollar went, and I would reevaluate the sheets and notes regularly—knowing exactly where my money was going enabled me to make more informed financial decisions and identify areas where I could cut back or save even more. Over time, even the smallest adjustments added up, and I regained a sense of control in the face of my challenges.

I developed the skill of financial discipline day by day, paycheck after paycheck. The more I practiced, the better I got at being resourceful in ways I didn't know I could. I was on the perpetual lookout for opportunities to cut costs, and one of my favorite methods was researching affordable alternatives for my living essentials. No one was as intentional about planning as I was. Seemingly small steps like preparing meals at home, opting for public transportation, and cutting back on non-essentials allowed me to focus my limited resources on what mattered most.

However, financial strain unavoidably took a mental toll that was difficult to ignore. The pressure of covering my basic needs and balancing my expenses while staying focused on my short-term and long-term goals was inevitably overwhelming. Giving in to the frustration and settling for less would have been easy at the time, but I embraced the financial challenges as a part of my journey. I even saw it as a test of persistence and resilience that I needed to pass to unlock the next level of my transformation in America. Thankfully, reframing the situation inside my head made pushing through the tough moments easier without derailing my focus.

I learned through all of this that financial stability entails more than figures and numbers. One must carefully craft a mindset sturdy enough to withstand all kinds of pressure. My decision to remain committed to my financial goals, despite money being incredibly tight, reinforced my firm belief that this phase was nothing but temporary. I was quite confident that I wasn't making all of these sacrifices in vain; rather, they were a way of investing in a future where I wouldn't have to worry about living paycheck to paycheck.

These experiences helped me establish a foundation that will serve me well in my new career. Budgeting, discipline, resilience, etc., have empowered me to approach my career with a sharp focus and a great appreciation for the opportunities I found later on my journey. I learned valuable lessons that have shaped my journey and how I approach work, money, and progress.

As you begin this new journey, the point is that you must cultivate a mindset that goes beyond managing money and embrace one that can empower you to overcome challenges and stay focused on your goals.

Learn to be resourceful, strategic, and resilient, and you'll have no problem turning financial struggles into stepping stones that bring you closer to the life you want with each intentional choice and decision.

The Steep Learning Curve in Cybersecurity

One thing you can expect from transitioning into cybersecurity is that it'll come with a learning curve unlike anything you've experienced before. Ambition isn't enough to break into this field due to the technicality of the industry. As I've previously noted, you will need a specific skill set and knowledge, which means the path won't be easy. So, prepare for a steep climb.

A major challenge I faced in the beginning was grasping the basics. As someone without a strong IT background veering into a field built on layers of technical knowledge for the first time, learning the foundational concepts was like learning a new language. Remember that this is normal and doesn't affect your chances as a non-technical person.

In the early phase, I encountered terms, systems, and practices that were new and unfamiliar to me, but those in the field seemed to know. At times, I'd feel like I was light years behind everyone else, and the sheer volume of information I needed to learn seemed daunting. Getting certified as a newbie wasn't a small feat. Different certifications had different requirements, and there were vast topics I was unfamiliar with. The material, ranging from network security to risk management, was dense and overwhelming.

Staying motivated in the face of all this was particularly hard for me. This wasn't a field where one could just skim the surface;

success could only be achieved through a full commitment to understanding each concept. At this point, imposter syndrome even set in for me. I thought, "Maybe this field is for people with years of experience, not someone trying to break in from scratch."

As you might expect, there were plenty of setbacks along the way. It's only natural. For instance, retaining information was sometimes a struggle when preparing for exams, and certain topics took twice as long to understand. I took some mock tests, but I didn't pass on the first attempt. Still, I considered the setbacks a part of the process rather than letting them deter me. Every failure came with a lesson about the material, and the struggle pushed me to refine my study strategies to the utmost level. Soon, I had mastered the art of breaking down the most complex topics into easy-to-digest bits by focusing on section after section. Initially, I'd try to master everything at once, but I learned to build my knowledge base layer by layer, which was quite effective.

During this journey, I stumbled across the concept of a growth mindset, which I'll share with you in depth later in the book. The idea of a growth mindset is to adopt lifelong learning and start viewing obstacles as opportunities to improve yourself rather than signs of incapability. You don't need to know everything at once—no one does. There will be progress as long as you keep learning and moving forward.

Adopting the growth mindset and attitude was a major game-changer. It allowed me to understand that mastery takes time.

I want you to know now that the steep learning curve in cybersecurity isn't something to fear. Think of it as a key part of entering a rigorous field like cybersecurity. Every hour you spend studying and every concept that eventually clicks because of your dedication can only bring you a step closer to your goal. With hard work and persistence, you can overcome any barrier, whether in unfamiliar territory or not.

Dealing with Setbacks and Learning from Failure

You might wonder, "*Why is he telling me about his struggles?*" Well, because I want you to know that there are obstacles and setbacks on every path to success, moments when things don't go as planned, and you start to doubt yourself. For this reason, you'll need resilience to keep going even when things go wrong.

Some moments will test your commitment and force you to confront failure head-on. That doesn't mean you've reached the end of the road. You need to seize those moments as opportunities to adjust, learn, and push forward with even greater determination.

One of the earliest setbacks I faced was during a major certification exam that I didn't pass. I remember feeling defeated and sinking, thinking that perhaps this was where I'd hop off the cybersecurity train. I found shaking the disappointment harder than normal, making me question everything. Was all this effort worth it? Was I fooling myself by thinking I could succeed here?

But as I processed that failure, I realized that my response to it would define my path forward. There were two choices before me: I could let the setback convince me to give up or let it fuel me. I chose the latter and returned to the study materials with a fresh perspective. I focused on the areas where I struggled the most and took my time to break down complex topics to understand them thoroughly before attempting the exam again. It wasn't easy.

When I came across a difficult concept, I would remind myself that mastery was a gradual process that took time. All I wanted to do was learn and improve myself.

During the job application process, another setback threatened my ambition. Despite investing hours upon hours into tailoring my resume and practicing interview skills, I faced a series of hurtful rejections. Every "no" felt so personal, as if the people in the industry were telling me that I didn't belong. But I quickly readjusted my view—rejection is an expected part of the journey. While someone else might have viewed these rejections as a reflection of their abilities, I saw them as feedback to analyze and improve upon. I used the failed interviews to identify areas where I could improve and adapted my approach based on what I learned. As such, each rejection made me more prepared, knowledgeable, and persistent.

If there's a lesson I hold dearly from the many setbacks I have overcome, success doesn't require perfection; it requires trying repeatedly. You don't have to fear or avoid failure. Instead, consider it a teacher guiding you toward self-development and growth.

Be eager to face challenges because they can only equip you to handle the next one better. Like me, learn to see setbacks as stepping stones rather than roadblocks. See each 'no' and failed attempt as a redirection meant to refine your path.

Overcoming those setbacks wasn't easy, but essential for my growth. Those experiences taught me to adapt myself and stay focused in uncertainty. I now consider failure a vital tool for sharpening my skills and strengthening my resolve. Without the failures I bounced back from, I may not have the same depth of knowledge and mental strength that have gotten me to where I am. Failure taught me to see challenges as temporary and to trust that persistence would lead me to success.

See failure not as something to avoid but as something to learn from. Success isn't about never failing; it's about getting back up every time you do, using each challenge as fuel to move forward.

Looking back, each obstacle I overcame critically contributed to my growth. I learned resourcefulness and discipline from my financial struggles. The cultural adjustments pushed me to be more open-minded and adaptable. The steep learning curve in cybersecurity demanded relentless dedication, while the mental barriers I overcame strengthened my resilience. Every odds I challenged brought me closer to the person I needed to become to succeed.

Now, I know every difficulty carries a lesson, and there isn't a straight path to success. The path is built on your ability to stay on track and keep moving forward, even if it feels like everything is against you. Rising above these challenges didn't just help me reach my goals; it prepared me for the journey ahead and gave me the confidence to tackle new obstacles as they came.

As I continue to build my career, these lessons stay with me, reminding me that resilience is one of the most valuable tools you can possess. Overcoming challenges doesn't end once you reach a certain level of success. It is a lifelong skill that allows you to keep growing, regardless of where you are on your journey.

What's Next?

As I tackled the hurdles of building a new life, I realized that the greatest obstacles weren't external. They lived within me—doubts, fears, and insecurities that threatened to hold me back even as I moved forward. Hidden barriers often go unnoticed on the path to success but can quietly sabotage even the best-laid plans. Knowing this, it is crucial to master the internal battles that can hold you back from reaching your potential. In the next chapter, I'll explore how I confronted these mental barriers and redefined my limits. More importantly, I will show you the profound mindset shifts that helped me break free from self-doubt and build the mental foundation necessary for lasting success. This is where the journey turns inward—because to overcome the world, you must first overcome yourself.

Facing Doubts: The Mental Barriers that Hold You Back

Addressing self-doubt, fear of failure, and staying motivated when challenges feel overwhelming.

When you set out to change your life, it's easy to see the external challenges you'll have to overcome. However, the hardest battles happen in your own mind. By this, I mean the internal fighting—the doubts and insecurities—that threaten to halt your progress before you begin. These mental barriers are some of the toughest obstacles to face because they don't announce themselves as clearly as the external ones. They linger quietly in the background, sometimes surfacing as a hesitant thought or a brief moment of doubt, only to sink deeper and make themselves comfortable.

Imagine preparing for a major step forward, perhaps an exam, a crucial interview, or a big decision that could change your life, only to hear that small voice in your mind saying, "Are you sure you're ready for this?" That voice doesn't need to shout. It plants a seed of doubt that grows quickly, rooting itself in every corner of your mind. Soon, you're questioning if you're truly capable or if you're cut out for this path at all. You might even find yourself standing on the edge of a promising opportunity, held back by a fear you can't quite name but feel deeply.

These doubts and the fear of failure are not obstacles that can be overcome with physical effort alone. They require a different kind of strength that isn't built overnight. In my case, I realized that facing these internal barriers was as critical, if not more so, than tackling any external hurdle in my path. Therefore, I was deliberate about mastering the thoughts and beliefs that could either drive me forward or hold me back.

This part of the journey is where I want us to discuss these internal battles that often accompany ambitious goals, from self-doubt and imposter syndrome to the deep-rooted fear of failure. They are universal yet deeply personal mental barriers. You will see the weight they carry, the strategies I used to push through them, and the insights that helped me transform these barriers into personal stepping stones. Because at the end of the day, the biggest battles we fight aren't with the world around us; they are the ones that take place in our minds.

The Weight of Self-Doubt: Recognizing Limiting Beliefs

Self-doubt has a quiet, persistent way of creeping in without making a grand entrance. I am certain it gets a kick out of showing up in those small moments when we're about to take a step forward, decide, or try something new. It whispers into the mind, "Are you sure you're ready?" "Do you really think you're good enough?" This voice doesn't need to be loud to have an impact. All it has to do is plant seeds that grow into a steady stream of limiting beliefs that hold us back from reaching our full potential.

It's a common struggle not constrained to you and me. Some of the most successful people in history have faced crushing self-doubt, but they persevered and pulled through. Take J.K. Rowling, for example, who once said, "I stopped pretending to myself that I was anything other than what I was and began to direct all my energy into finishing the only work that mattered to me." Rowling faced years of rejection, financial struggle, and relentless self-doubt before becoming one of the best-selling authors in history despite the odds stacked against her. Like a soldier, she found a way to keep writing, even when it felt like no one else believed in her work.

Self-doubt often has deep roots, such as past experiences, moments when we felt we weren't enough, or comparing ourselves to others who seem more successful. Other times, it's shaped by societal expectations, which make us feel like we have to follow a certain path or meet certain standards to be "successful." These beliefs often gradually take hold unnoticed and become part of our internal dialogue. The problem is, if left unchecked, they become a pattern—a default reaction whenever we face a challenge.

I can't recollect all the times when self-doubt nearly stopped me along my journey, but I assure you they were numerous. The more I worked toward building a cybersecurity career, the more I felt like an imposter trying to fit in where I didn't belong. One particular incident stands out vividly in my mind. I had an upcoming interview for a role that I had been working tirelessly to qualify for, but as I prepared, that familiar voice popped into my head again: "Are you sure you're good enough?" it whispered. "What if they see right through you?"

No matter how many hours I spent studying, rehearsing my responses, and doing everything I could to prepare, that nagging voice was inside my head, trying hard to convince me that my best efforts wouldn't be enough.

This feeling is far from unique. Albert Einstein, one of the most brilliant minds of all time, reportedly felt like an imposter throughout his career. Despite his groundbreaking work, he once admitted, "The exaggerated esteem in which my lifework is held makes me very ill at ease. I feel compelled to think of myself as an involuntary swindler." If someone as accomplished as Einstein could experience self-doubt, it's clear that this feeling doesn't discriminate; it's something that even the most accomplished individuals grapple with.

Recognizing self-doubt is the first step to moving past it. One of the most effective ways to disarm it is by identifying it as a pattern of thought, not a truth. Self-doubt can be powerful, but only if we accept it as fact. I began to realize that I had a choice when faced with self-doubt. I could let it hold me back or confront it and move forward despite it.

A practical strategy I learned was to question my own thoughts. Instead of accepting that voice as truth, I began to ask myself: "Is there real evidence for this doubt? What would I tell a friend in my position?" Reframing my thoughts this way enabled me to step back and view self-doubt more objectively.

Also, I do this thing where I look at my past achievements, however small, and remind myself that I have already overcome challenges. These reminders helped to build confidence over time as they slowly chipped away at the limiting beliefs that had held me back.

I have found that a more compelling way of overcoming self-doubt is to find mentors, role models, or stories of others who have overcome similar feelings. Seeing how others have succeeded despite their doubts is a powerful reminder that I am not alone in challenging limiting beliefs. When I read stories of successful figures, I realized that self-doubt is simply part of the journey. More importantly, it shows me that the difference between those who succeed and those who don't often comes down to resilience, i.e., whether they choose to act in the face of fear or uncertainty.

Self-doubt may always be present, but it doesn't have to define the path forward. It's not about never feeling uncertain; it's about learning to move forward anyway. Each time we face self-doubt, we gain an opportunity to strengthen our resilience and trust in our abilities. Learning to challenge those limiting beliefs, rather than giving them power, is the first step in turning that inner critic into a quiet background noise rather than the loud voice steering the course of our lives.

Imposter Syndrome: Overcoming the Feeling of Not Belonging

You are probably familiar with the concept of imposter syndrome. It's a feeling that goes beyond simple self-doubt in the sense that you, somehow, find yourself thinking that you don't deserve the successes you've achieved, that you're "faking it" and will soon be found out. This is especially true for anyone pursuing a new path or career, particularly in highly technical or competitive fields. Imposter syndrome has a way of making even the most capable people question their abilities. These thoughts often surface the more a person progresses and makes something of themselves.

That's when you'll catch the inner critic whispering, "You don't really belong here. You're just pretending."

The feeling of being an imposter isn't unique to beginners. Many most accomplished figures have spoken openly about experiencing this very thing. For example, Maya Angelou, who wrote multiple bestsellers and received numerous awards, once admitted, "I have written eleven books, but each time I think, 'Uh oh, they're going to find out now. I've run a game on everybody, and they're going to find me out.'" Hearing this from a figure as revered as Angelou is a powerful reminder that feeling like an imposter is a part of the journey for many people, even those at the top of their fields.

For me, imposter syndrome first appeared when I started to make real progress in cybersecurity. I'd land interviews, secure certifications, and even receive positive feedback, but that inner voice never let up. Instead of celebrating, I'd find myself thinking, "They must have made a mistake," or "If they knew how much I don't know, they'd never take me seriously." For a while, this didn't just affect my confidence; it impacted how I viewed my own achievements. No matter how many hurdles I overcame, there was always this lingering belief that I didn't belong.

One reason imposter syndrome is so pervasive is that it often stems from high personal standards and the desire to be competent. Many of us believe that success should come effortlessly to truly talented people. But in reality, growth is rarely smooth, and the journey is often full of setbacks and learning curves. This internal disconnect between what we think "real" success looks like, and the actual messy path to achievement can deepen imposter syndrome. People like Howard Schultz, the former CEO of Starbucks, also expressed their feelings this way: "Very few people, whether you've been in that job before or not, get into the seat and believe today that they are now qualified."

Learning to manage imposter syndrome took me a substantial amount of time and a deliberate shift in perspective. One of the first things I did was recognize it for what it is. Feeling like an imposter doesn't mean you are because feelings aren't facts. It helps to constantly remind yourself that imposter syndrome isn't a reflection of your abilities but a mental pattern many people face. Identifying it is necessary to separate the feeling from your identity.

Another powerful approach I learned is to reframe how I view mistakes or gaps in knowledge. Imposter syndrome thrives on the idea that one should already know everything, and any gaps signal incompetence. However, taking time to examine every challenge as part of a broader learning process makes it incredibly easier to accept those gaps as normal. When I used this approach, over time, I started to view new challenges not as proof that I didn't belong but as proof that I was growing. This mindset shift didn't eliminate imposter syndrome overnight but made those feelings less overpowering.

Simply talking about imposter syndrome was another helpful strategy. Imposter syndrome feeds off isolation and silence, convincing you that you're the only one struggling. But as soon as you begin sharing your experiences, you realize how common this feeling really is. Many mentors, colleagues, and friends opened up about their own struggles, which made me feel less alone. Knowing that others had gone through the same doubts was incredibly reassuring.

Consider actress and writer Tina Fey, who humorously addressed imposter syndrome by saying, "The beauty of the imposter syndrome is you vacillate between extreme egomania and a complete feeling of, 'I'm a fraud! Oh God, they're on to me! I'm a fraud!'" Fey's humor highlights a truth many of us face: the highs and lows are part of the human experience. We aren't frauds—we're just learning, evolving, and occasionally stumbling as we grow.

Ultimately, the goal isn't to eliminate imposter syndrome completely. It's about learning to live with it without letting it define you. I realized that every time I pushed forward despite those feelings, I reshaped my self-image, proving to myself that I belonged. It wasn't about "faking it till I made it." Instead, it was about recognizing that confidence comes from action, from moving forward even when self-doubt tries to hold you back.

The bottom line is that imposter syndrome is a universal experience affecting people from all walks of life. By acknowledging it, reframing mistakes as part of growth, and connecting with others who share the same feelings, you can begin to take ownership of your achievements.

Fear of Failure: Learning to Embrace Risks

Fear is an interesting thing. It feels ancient, wired into us to protect against the worst, yet it often shows up in the least threatening moments. Fear of failure, in particular, thrives where ambition meets uncertainty. It grows in the space between what we hope to achieve and what we risk by trying. It's not the kind of fear that comes from danger; it's quieter and more persistent. That voice in your head asks, "What if they see you stumble?"

As I've come to realize, failure is more than an event; it is a reflection. We fear it not only for the immediate consequences but also for what it seems to say about who we are. The job we didn't get or the idea that didn't land can feel like a judgment or a statement that we're not good enough. That fear can be paralyzing, which convinces us that staying safe is better than trying.

But the irony is that failure is so often a prerequisite for success. Think about how absurd it would be to avoid exercising because the initial soreness might feel like failure. In any form, growth requires discomfort, missteps, and moments where your limits are exposed. Unfortunately, we give failure an outsized meaning amplified by a culture that publicly celebrates wins and quietly dismisses struggles.

The fear of failure was a constant companion early in my journey. I knew the stakes were high, and that voice in my head was always ready to remind me of the risks. What if I failed that certification exam? What if I flubbed an interview? What if my effort didn't match the result? Each step forward felt like stepping into a spotlight where every mistake would be magnified. At times, I hesitated, not because I didn't believe in the process but because I feared what failure might say about me.

That fear didn't just affect me—it shaped how I approached opportunities. I would overprepare to try and eliminate any chance of mistakes, only to find that perfectionism was just another way of hiding. I had to unlearn that mindset and retrain my mind to see failure as proof of my effort rather than a symbol of my inadequacy. I stopped seeing it as a final verdict but an essential checkpoint in my growth.

Look at someone like Steve Jobs, who was famously removed from Apple, the company he co-founded. For most people, that kind of public setback would have been devastating. Jobs, however, used that time to refine his ideas and ultimately return to Apple stronger, which enabled him to reshape the company into the global leader we know today. His story is one of resilience because he chose to see failure as a pivot point rather than a dead end.

I started reframing failure by changing how I viewed it. Instead of seeing it as a monster waiting to devour my confidence, I treated it like feedback. Any failed attempt at something—a pitch, a test, even a conversation—wasn't evidence of incompetence; it was a signal of what needed refining. Whenever I stumbled, I asked myself, "What does this teach me?" That simple question turned failure from an enemy into a teacher.

Another thing I learned was the power of vulnerability. Failure feels heavier when you carry it alone. Early on, I thought admitting mistakes would make me seem weak or unprepared, but the truth is that sharing your failures can be incredibly freeing. I realized how universal failure is when I opened up to mentors, peers, and friends about my struggles. No one gets it right the first time, and pretending otherwise only isolates you. Vulnerability isn't weakness; it is honesty that fosters connection in ways that perfection never can.

The most important lesson, though, was realizing that failure is temporary. Its sting fades, but its lessons remain. Each failure chipped away at my fear and left something stronger in its place: resilience. Progress isn't linear; it loops and stumbles before surging forward. Fearing failure is like fearing the very nature of growth itself. Without it, there's no learning, no evolution, no transformation.

If fear of failure is holding you back, it's time to rethink what failure really means. It isn't the end of the road—it's a part of the journey. It's not a judgment of your abilities; it's a tool for refining them. Embrace failure as feedback, open yourself to vulnerability, and remember that every stumble carries a lesson so that you can move forward with courage. The question isn't whether you'll fail. The question is whether you'll use that failure to become something greater.

Strategies for Building Mental Resilience

Resilience is one of those concepts that sounds simple until you are forced to live it. It is easy to talk about bouncing back when life feels manageable, but the real test comes in those quiet moments of defeat when getting back up feels more like a negotiation with yourself than a natural response. I now know from experience that resilience is not a fixed trait but a skill, like learning to swim in a choppy ocean. The waves will always come, but you learn to keep your head above water with practice.

My experiences with failure have helped me to start understanding resilience differently. It is less about being impervious to setbacks and more about learning to sit with discomfort and ask what it teaches you. I have learned to see resilience as the ability to reframe failure as a data point rather than as judgment. Like an experiment that yields unexpected results, failure offers insight, even when it stings. This shift in perspective transformed the way I approached challenges.

One of the most practical tools I adopted was journaling. It sounds simple, even mundane, but writing became a way to make sense of the chaos in my mind. I didn't use my journal as a place for polished thoughts; it was raw, filled with frustrations, doubts, and half-formed ideas. But in that mess, patterns started to emerge where I could see what triggered my doubts, what strategies worked, and where I was getting in my own way. Journaling was a mirror that showed me parts of myself I had overlooked.

I also used a strategy that I call "micro-recovery," and it proved invaluable. We often associate resilience with major comebacks, but the truth is that it is built in the small moments. For instance, I didn't immediately sign up for the next one after the failed exam I told you about. Instead, I gave myself time to regroup and spent a week reviewing where I had struggled, not as an act of self-punishment but as a way to prepare differently. I took breaks when my focus waned and trusted that rest was part of the process. These small acts of recovery added up and created a foundation of strength I could draw on when I tried again.

Visualization was also incredibly helpful, especially on days when progress felt impossible. In those moments, I would close my eyes and imagine the version of myself I was working toward. I pictured sitting in an office where my contributions mattered and I could solve challenging problems, knowing I had earned my place. This wasn't wishful thinking; it reminded me why I started. Visualization gave me a focal point and a way to pull my thoughts away from the fear of failing again toward the future I was building.

Keep in mind that you cannot build resilience in isolation. Faith was an anchor for me through it all. It offered a perspective larger than my immediate struggles because I found a purpose beyond passing an exam or landing a job whenever I prayed or reflected spiritually. Faith reminded me that my journey was part of something bigger and that even the setbacks had meaning. I was confident that if I didn't avoid the struggle, it would shape me into someone stronger.

I want you always to remind yourself that resilience isn't a finish line to cross. Rather, it is a way of being that you can build piece by piece through intentional choices. It is the decision to get back up, even when unsure of the outcome. It is trusting that the effort will pay off, not immediately, but eventually.

Resilience may not make this journey easier, but it makes you better equipped to handle its twists and turns—and that, ultimately, is what carries you forward.

If there's one thing I've learned, the battles we fight in our minds shape us more than any external challenge ever could. Mental barriers, whether fear of failure, self-doubt, or imposter syndrome, are not signs of weakness. They're invitations for us to look deeper, question the stories we've told ourselves, and rewrite them with courage and clarity.

My doubts and fears still surface occasionally, but they no longer control the narrative because I learned to see them for what they are: stepping stones, not walls. They don't block the path; they reveal it.

What I want you to take with you is that these internal struggles are not the enemy. They're the training ground where you can learn persistence when the odds feel stacked against you. They teach you grace when you stumble, and most importantly, they remind you that growth comes from embracing the hard things, not avoiding them.

Your challenges are uniquely yours, but so is your ability to overcome them. Every time you face a barrier and push through, you're not just moving closer to your goals. You're becoming the person who can achieve them. That transformation is the real victory.

Mental barriers are not meant to stop you. They're meant to prepare you. With each doubt you confront, each fear you face, and each step you take, you're building a foundation of resilience that will carry you through whatever comes next.

What's Next?

By confronting the doubts and fears that held me back, I uncovered the clarity and strength to push forward. But resilience alone wasn't enough. It was time to channel that strength into focused effort and a clear vision for the future.

Overcoming mental barriers lays the foundation, but resilience alone doesn't complete the journey. What you do with that strength and how you channel it into focused effort and a clear vision determines how far you'll go. Hard work is the bridge that connects your potential to your goals, and vision is the compass that keeps you moving in the right direction.

In the next chapter, **The Power of Hard Work and Vision**, we'll explore how these two elements transformed my journey.

The Power of Hard Work and Vision

If resilience is the foundation, hard work and vision are the architecture of success. One gives you the tools to persist, and the other ensures you build in the right direction. Without both, you can spend years tirelessly climbing a ladder only to find it leaning against the wrong wall. That realization can be sobering, and it was for me.

When I first began my journey, I believed hard work alone would take me to where I wanted to go. It felt intuitive—work harder, do more, and eventually get there. But "there" is a vague destination. Without a clear sense of what I was working toward, I found myself putting in hours, sacrificing weekends, and chasing every opportunity without asking the critical question: Does this align with what I truly want? It was like I had a shovel and endless energy but no map.

Vision changed that for me by giving my effort a purpose. Vision isn't just about setting goals or dreaming big. It is about understanding why those goals matter and how they fit into the larger picture of your life. Having a clear vision acts as a filter that helps you decide what deserves your time and energy. It doesn't eliminate hard work and ensures that your hard work moves you forward instead of in circles.

But vision alone isn't enough. We often romanticize the power of ideas and imagine that clarity of purpose will carry us effortlessly to success. In reality, vision without action is daydreaming, and hard work, with all its grind and grit, is what transforms ideas into outcomes. The late nights spent studying, the uncomfortable conversations where you advocate for yourself, the quiet hours dedicated to practice—these moments don't look glamorous but are where progress lives.

The truth is hard work and vision are interdependent. One without the other is incomplete, as you'll see in a subsequent part of this chapter. Vision without effort is empty ambition, and hard work without vision is wasted energy. Together, they are unstoppable.

As we move through this chapter, I want you to reflect on your own journey. Are you putting in the work? And just as importantly, do you know where it is leading you? Success is not about choosing between effort and purpose. It is about mastering the balance between the two.

What Hard Work Really Means

Hard work is one of those phrases we toss around so often that it loses meaning. It becomes a cliché, a banner under which everyone marches, even when no one agrees on what it actually entails. We're told to work hard, but no one talks about what that really looks like. Is it about the number of hours you put in, the intensity of your focus, or the sacrifices you make along the way? And perhaps most importantly, does working hard guarantee success?

These were the questions I wrestled with early on, and the answers were more complicated than I expected.

Let's start with a hard truth: hard work is essential but not sufficient. There are countless stories of people who worked tirelessly but never got their break. That reality can feel disheartening if you let it, but it is also liberating. It means that hard work is not just about effort but about direction, discipline, and discernment. The work itself matters, but so does the way you approach it.

When I think about hard work, I think about those early days when I was juggling multiple jobs to keep myself afloat. Deliveries in the evening, factory shifts on weekends, and late nights spent trying to learn the basics of cybersecurity. It was exhausting, but it wasn't aimless—each task taught me something, no matter how unrelated it seemed. The deliveries taught me efficiency, the factory work taught me patience, and the hours spent learning cybersecurity taught me resilience. Hard work is rarely glamorous, but it is always revealing. It shows you what you are made of and what you are willing to endure for what you want.

There is a cultural obsession with shortcuts and with finding the hack that will make success come faster or easier. This mindset is seductive because it promises results without the struggle, but shortcuts are often just distractions in disguise. They pull you away from the work that matters and leave you with half-finished projects and a nagging sense of incompleteness. I've learned that hard work is about both speed and consistency. It shows up every day, even when the results are invisible, and trusts that the process will eventually pay off.

One of the biggest myths about hard work is that it looks the same for everyone. When we think about hard work, we tend to visualize the image of the tireless entrepreneur who survives on coffee and three hours of sleep, as if suffering is the only indicator of effort. But hard work is personal. Personally, it meant learning to balance my energy, prioritizing tasks that aligned with my goals, and saying no to distractions disguised as opportunities. I learned the importance of being intentional with my time and effort instead of burning myself out to prove my worth.

Serena Williams' dominance in tennis is often attributed to her work ethic, but that doesn't mean she spends every waking moment on the court. Her hard work is deliberate. It includes intense training, yes, but also rest, recovery, and mental preparation. Hard work is less about what you do and more about how you do it. It is the difference between running aimlessly and running with a destination in mind.

In my own journey, discipline was the hardest part of hard work to master. It is easy to be motivated initially when the goal feels new and exciting, but what happens when the excitement fades, and all you are left with is the grind? That is where discipline comes in. It keeps you going when motivation wavers and makes you put in the work even when progress feels nonexistent. Discipline is not glamorous, but it transforms effort into results.

Hard work also requires the humility to recognize what you don't know and be willing to learn, even when it feels uncomfortable. Early in my career, I had to swallow my pride and ask for help from more experienced people, which wasn't easy but necessary. Hard is about doing better, not more, and sometimes, that means admitting that you can't do it all on your own.

If there is one thing I want you to take away, it is this: hard work is not a magic bullet but a non-negotiable part of the journey. It is the foundation upon which everything else is built. Success may not always come to those who work hard, but it rarely comes without it. You need hard work to become someone who can achieve your goals.

I want you to know that even though hard work is not a guarantee, it is a catalyst. It is not just about effort but about intention, discipline, and persistence. It is not about working more; it is about working smarter. Most importantly, it is about showing up for yourself every day, even when the path ahead feels uncertain. In the end, the work you put in shapes not just your outcomes but who you are.

The Role of Vision in Shaping Your Path

We tend to confuse vision with ambition or goals, but it is quite different. Vision extends beyond what you want to achieve to why you want to achieve it. It is a compass that guides your decisions and helps you navigate the chaos of daily life. Without it, hard work can feel like running in circles and expending energy without moving forward.

I had no shortage of ambition when I got to the United States. In fact, I was brimming with it because I wanted more than I had and was willing to work for it. What I lacked was clarity. I was chasing opportunities without understanding how they connected to the bigger picture, which felt like building a puzzle without knowing what the final image would look like. I kept busy, but my busyness was not the same as my progress.

In this regard, vision changed everything for me by giving my work direction. It turned my efforts into something deliberate with purpose. You don't have to dream big or set unrealistic goals to have a vision. You need to see beyond the immediate task at hand and understand how it fits into the broader story you are trying to write. That is the pivotal difference between working for a paycheck and working toward a life you believe in.

Take the example of Elon Musk, whose vision for SpaceX was to build rockets and make life multi-planetary. That clarity of purpose continues to shape every decision he makes, from the risks he was willing to take to the people he brought onto his team. Whether or not you agree with his methods, there is no denying the power of a sharp vision—it cuts through distractions and focuses energy on what matters most.

Vision is not static; it evolves as you do. The vision I had when I first started out is not the same as the one I hold today. Back then, it was about surviving and creating a stable foundation. Now, it is about growth, impact, and leaving something behind that matters. Vision grows with you and expands as you achieve the things you once only dreamed of.

The truth is that vision is not about eliminating struggle. It is about making the struggle meaningful. It gives you something to hold onto when progress is slow, and the challenges feel insurmountable. It reminds you why you started and why it is worth continuing.

One of the greatest challenges to maintaining vision is the noise. We live in a world where everyone is chasing something, and it is easy to get swept up in other people's agendas. Social media compounds this by presenting a curated version of success that makes you question your own path. This is where vision becomes critical in acting as a filter that can help you separate what is important from what is not. This keeps you anchored, even when the world tries to pull you in a hundred different directions.

To cultivate my vision, I had to take the time to reflect. I would spend quiet evenings asking myself questions that felt deceptively simple. What do I want? Why does it matter? What am I willing to sacrifice to get there? These questions were not easy to answer, but they forced me to confront what I truly valued and helped me see past the distractions to focus on what really mattered.

Vision also requires courage. It is not enough to see the path; you must be willing to walk it, even when it feels lonely or uncertain. Vision asks you to trust yourself and believe in the picture you are building, whether it is complete or not. You don't need all the answers but must have faith in the process.

The bottom line is that vision is a necessity that gives your work purpose and your life direction. It helps you make decisions that align with your values and keeps you moving forward when the road gets tough. Vision is not about predicting the future; it is about creating it. That starts with the willingness to see beyond the present moment and imagine what could be.

The Intersection of Hard Work and Vision

Hard work and vision are like two musicians playing a duet. One provides a steady and persistent rhythm, while the other carries the melody, imaginative and forward-looking. The harmony falls apart without either, but together, they create something extraordinary. This interplay is deeply human, and we see it in every story of success that marries effort with purpose.

I often think of someone like Daniel, whose story reflects the reality I have witnessed time and again. Daniel was a factory worker who dreamed of becoming a software engineer without formal training, a tech degree, or an outline. He had a vision to create a better life for himself and his family, one where his work felt meaningful and his time was valued. That vision lit a fire within him that wasn't enough on its own, so he found a way to translate that dream into reality.

Daniel started small. After his shifts at the factory, he would sit at a borrowed laptop in his tiny apartment and teach himself the basics of programming. The work was grueling, and his friends laughed at him while his family worried he was wasting his time. Some nights, exhaustion got the better of him, but most nights, he pushed through.

His vision kept Daniel going, which wasn't abstract or distant. He could see it clearly in his mind—the kind of work he wanted to do, the people he wanted to surround himself with, and the freedom he wanted to achieve. That clarity turned his hard work into something more than effort. It became an investment.

But, as you now know, vision is not a straight line, and hard work is rarely predictable. Daniel faced setbacks. He failed his first coding boot camp. He struggled to understand certain concepts and doubted whether he could make such a massive career shift. It would have been easy to quit by convincing himself that he had aimed too high. Instead, he leaned on his vision and used it as a compass to guide his next steps.

Daniel adjusted his approach. He sought out free resources online, joined a community of aspiring programmers, and found a mentor who had walked a similar path. Each decision was born out of the alignment between his vision and his effort. Slowly but surely, his work began to bear fruit. He built his first app, then another. A year later, he landed his first internship in tech.

The story of someone like Daniel is not extraordinary because of its outcome. It is extraordinary because of the journey. It illustrates the power of combining hard work and vision. Hard work kept him moving when progress was slow, while vision ensured that each step he took brought him closer to the life he wanted. Together, they created a momentum that transformed his future.

The lesson here is not just about perseverance; it is also about balance. Hard work without vision is like rowing without a destination, and vision without hard work is like standing on the shore, dreaming of distant lands but never setting sail. The magic happens at their intersection, where effort fuels purpose, and purpose gives meaning to effort.

Despite feeling the weight of uncertainty and the pull of self-doubt on my own path, I, like Daniel, found that when hard work and vision align, they create a kind of resilience that no setback can shake. Hard work is the engine that keeps you going, while vision is the map that shows you where to go. One without the other leaves you either stuck or lost.

If you are reading this and wondering how to align your own effort with your purpose, start by asking yourself: What does success look like to me? What am I willing to work for? And how can I ensure that my work leads me closer to what I value most? These questions are not easy, but they are essential. They turn vague ambition into deliberate action, and action is where transformation begins.

Like Daniel, you can align your effort with your purpose, creating a path that reflects who you are and who you want to become.

Practical Strategies for Refining Your Vision

Refining your vision is an evolving process that requires introspection, action, and flexibility. Vision grows as you grow, shaped by your experiences and the lessons you learn along the way.

Here are practical strategies to help you refine and strengthen your vision:

Start with questions.

Begin by asking yourself meaningful questions that go beyond surface-level goals.

- What do I truly want, and why does it matter to me?
- How does this vision align with my values and the person I want to become?
- Am I pursuing this vision for myself or because of external expectations?

These questions clarify your motivation and help you differentiate between meaningful goals and distractions.

Treat vision as a process.

Vision is not something you figure out all at once. It develops through action and reflection.

- Take a small step toward what you think you want.
- Evaluate how that step feels and what it teaches you about

your goals.

- Use these insights to adjust your vision as needed.

Each action you take adds another piece to the puzzle and sharpens your sense of purpose.

Embrace reflection. Reflection creates the space needed for your vision to grow. Regularly ask yourself:

- What felt meaningful today?
- What drained my energy or distracted me?
- What am I working toward, and does it still resonate?

These daily or weekly reflections provide clarity over time, which will help you refine your goals and stay connected to your purpose.

Visualize your future.

Visualization is a powerful tool for refining vision. Picture the life you want to create in broad strokes and great detail.

- What does a successful day look like?
- How does your work align with your values?
- What kind of relationships and experiences define this life?

Use these mental images to guide your decisions, ensuring they align with your long-term aspirations.

Stay open to change. Vision evolves. What matters to you today may shift as you grow and gain new experiences.

- Revisit your goals regularly to ensure they still reflect your priorities.
- Allow your vision to expand as you achieve milestones, keeping it aligned with who you are becoming.

Flexibility is not a weakness. It is a sign of growth.

Leverage community.

Surround yourself with people who challenge, inspire, and support you.

- Seek mentors who can provide guidance and share their experiences.
- Engage with peers who are on similar journeys to gain new perspectives.
- Share your vision with others to create accountability and motivation.

A strong community acts as a mirror that can help you see your vision from angles you might have missed.

Act and iterate. Vision becomes clear through action, not overthinking. Start small, and let your experiences guide you.

- Try something new that aligns with your vision, even if it feels uncertain.
- Learn from the outcomes and refine your approach.
- Remember that experimentation is part of the process.

Each step forward, even a misstep, brings you closer to a vision that feels authentic and achievable.

With the right strategies and a willingness to take deliberate steps, your vision can become a guide and a source of inspiration for everything you do.

Now, keep in mind that vision alone is not enough. It is the spark that ignites the journey, but hard work is what keeps the fire alive. The challenge lies in bridging the gap between what you see in your mind and what exists in the world. That space between dreaming and doing is where most people falter. It is where fear, distractions, and self-doubt creep in, whispering that the work is too much and the dream is too far. But the truth is, that gap is where the magic happens.

I remember the first time I set a goal that truly scared me. It wasn't just ambitious; it felt impossible. I wanted to transition into a field I had no experience in, competing against people who had spent years honing their skills. It would have been easier to let the vision stay in my head, where it was safe and untouchable. But I knew that if I didn't take action, the vision would become a source of regret, not inspiration.

The hardest part was taking the first step. It wasn't glamorous or dramatic. It was small, like registering for an introductory course or committing to a few hours of study each night. These actions didn't feel transformative in the moment, but over time, they added up. The path from vision to reality is built through the accumulation of effort, knowledge, and resilience.

Turning a vision into reality also means being willing to fail. Remember what we said about failure: it is not the enemy of progress but a natural part of every process. Each misstep taught me something new that helped me refine my approach and adjust my expectations. The vision never changed, but the way I pursued it did. This brings me to another point: flexibility is as important as persistence. Without it, you risk clinging to a strategy that no longer serves you.

I've learned that vision gives you direction, but action gives you clarity. The more you do, the clearer the path becomes. The gap between where you are and where you want to be will never close on its own. You have to step into it, one deliberate choice at a time.

The point is that vision is your guide, but only action can bring it to life. The bridge between dreaming and doing is built with small, consistent steps, a willingness to adapt, and a resolve to keep moving forward.

What's Next?

Every vision realized, and every goal achieved carries a deeper story about the values, sacrifices, and perseverance that shape true success. But success is rarely what it seems on the surface. It's not just the accolades or the milestones; it's the journey of challenging perceptions, breaking molds, and redefining what success looks like for yourself.

That is precisely why I want us to explore how the path to success often defies convention in the next part of this book. Together, you and I will unpack the myths, the pressures, and the unexpected truths that come with forging your own definition of achievement.

Breaking Stereotypes: What Success Really Looks Like

There are a lot of misconceptions about what it means to be successful. Is it just about money? Status? This chapter breaks down common myths and helps redefine success on one's terms, grounded in purpose and personal fulfillment.

What does success mean to you? It is a deceptively simple question, yet the answers are often borrowed rather than created. For most of us, the idea of success begins to take shape long before we are aware of it, molded by the expectations of family, culture, and the invisible hands of society. When we start chasing it, we often find ourselves sprinting toward someone else's definition, only to feel empty when we finally arrive.

I used to believe that success was a checklist—a certain income, a specific job title, a life that looked good on paper. And for a while, I chased that vision, convinced it was the key to happiness. But something was always missing—every achievement felt fleeting, every milestone a momentary high before the inevitable crash of "what's next?" I began to realize that the problem wasn't in my effort; it was in my definition.

Society tells us a template for success, neatly packaged in prestige, wealth, and power. It promises fulfillment through external markers like degrees, promotions, and accolades, but success, as I have understood, is not something you can measure with numbers or display on a mantelpiece. It is not a finish line you cross or a trophy you hold. True success is deeply personal. It is a meaningful life because it is aligned with your values and true to your identity.

One of the most insidious traps of traditional success narratives is how they flatten the complexity of human experience. They ignore the paths that do not follow a linear trajectory or the dreams that do not fit neatly into conventional categories. Think about how often we judge success by the outward appearance of someone's life. The corner office, the luxury car, the curated vacation photos. But how often do we stop to ask whether those symbols represent joy, purpose, or authenticity?

It wasn't an easy process when I started redefining success for myself. It required peeling back layers of expectation and questioning what I had internalized as "normal." More importantly, I had to learn how to listen to the quiet voice that knew what I wanted.

This chapter is an invitation for you to do the same. I want you to pause and ask yourself whether the vision of success you are chasing is truly yours. I want you to let go of the metrics and milestones that do not serve you. Finally, I want you to imagine a version of success that feels expansive, dynamic, and deeply connected to who you are.

The problem with success, as it is often defined, is not just that it feels impersonal but assumes a single, universal path. This assumption creates a template that leaves little room for individuality, making it easy to feel out of place if your journey does not align with the supposed norm. But the truth is, there is no universal success story. What works for one person may feel stifling for another. Understanding this myth is the first step in breaking free from it.

The Myth of the Universal Success Story

When we talk about success, we often talk about it as if it is a universal experience—a singular story with predictable markers and a clear trajectory. A good education leads to a good job and a comfortable life. Stay on the track long enough to reach the golden conclusion: success. But life is a series of decisions, missteps, and redirections, often defined as much by what we endure as by what we achieve. And, as I have come to understand it, success is deeply personal.

The myth of the universal success story is everywhere, woven into our culture and perpetuated by systems that equate worth with productivity and wealth. In cybersecurity, for example, success is often portrayed as the domain of technical prodigies. People imagine hackers in hoodies or engineers with degrees from elite institutions who are effortlessly navigating a world of firewalls and algorithms. But this image is painfully narrow and erases the diversity of paths that lead to impactful careers in the field.

When I started my journey into cybersecurity, I did not fit the mold, as you know. I wasn't a computer science graduate or a lifelong tech enthusiast. My experience was rooted in persistence, curiosity, and an unrelenting desire to change my circumstances. I worked as a delivery driver, not because I loved the grind but because I needed to survive. Success began not with mastery but with humility, a willingness to learn, and the courage to start despite feeling like an outsider.

This myth of a singular path is not just misleading; it is limiting. It discourages people who do not see themselves reflected in the dominant narrative. How many potential innovators or problem-solvers are held back because they believe they lack the "right" background? How many people hesitate to pursue cybersecurity or any field because they are convinced their story does not align with the industry's expectations?

I have learned that success comes from expanding the mold rather than trying to fit within it. In cybersecurity, some of the most successful professionals are not traditional technologists. They bring unique perspectives to the table—teachers who excel in training teams, lawyers who navigate complex regulations, or creatives who design systems with empathy and user experience in mind. Their stories defy the myth of the universal success story and prove there is no single way to make an impact.

The problem with rigid success narratives is that they reduce complexity to simplicity. They turn a spectrum into a binary: you are either successful or not, in or out, worthy or lacking. This binary thinking ignores the nuances that make each journey unique and fails to account for the role of privilege, timing, and sheer unpredictability in shaping outcomes. It also overlooks the fact that success is a continuous process constantly reshaped by new goals, challenges, and definitions.

In cybersecurity, the idea of expanding success resonates deeply. The field thrives on diversity—not just of people but of perspectives. Cyber threats evolve because adversaries think creatively, which means the solutions to those threats must be just as innovative. This requires professionals who approach problems from different angles, question assumptions and see value in what others might overlook.

The myth of the universal success story is persistent because it is comforting. It gives us something to aspire to: a sense of order in a chaotic world. But real success is messier, nonlinear, unpredictable, and deeply human. We find it in the moments of struggle and self-discovery, the willingness to fail and try again, and the courage to define your worth on your own terms.

If there is one thing I hope to leave you with, it is this: your path is enough. It does not have to look like anyone else's. It does not have to fit neatly into a narrative written by someone who does not know your story. Success is a reality you create for yourself, one decision at a time, and it is not a myth to chase. The beauty of that is that no one else defines what it means for you.

Once we recognize that success cannot be boiled down to a single narrative, the next question becomes deeply personal: what does success mean for you? Stripping away societal expectations is not enough. You must also have the courage to craft your own definition that resonates with your values and aspirations. It is not about rejecting ambition but about aligning it with what truly matters to you.

Authentic Success: Defining It for Yourself

As much as success is one of the most personal concepts we encounter in life, we often let external voices dictate it. Parents, peers, social media, and even the industries we work in all contribute to a version of success that feels less like a choice and more like a mandate, but true success is something you define, refine, and own, not something you inherit.

Defining authentic success requires peeling back the layers of expectation, but not by rejecting ambition or ignoring external rewards because those things still have value. However, this is only when they are in alignment with your deeper sense of purpose. Personally, my alignment came when I stopped asking, "What do I want to achieve?" and started asking, "Why does it matter?" That simple shift changed everything and forced me to evaluate the life I was building around the goals I was pursuing.

In cybersecurity, success often takes on dimensions that transcend traditional metrics. Beyond the certifications and titles, the true measure lies in the unseen, such as safeguarding systems that millions rely on without ever knowing. Success in this field doesn't have to be entirely about what you achieve for yourself. It can also be about the security and trust you create for others. A kind of quiet confidence comes from knowing your work has made the digital world just a little safer, even if one of the most liberating realizations I had was that success is not a competition. It is easy to fall into the trap of comparing your journey to someone else's, especially in a field like cybersecurity, where achievements are often quantified. Certifications, salaries, and even the prestige of the companies you work for can become yardsticks for self-worth, but as the saying goes, comparison is a thief. It steals your focus, confidence, and ability to see your own path's unique value.

Authentic success requires courage. It is difficult to step away from the crowd and say, "This is what matters to me, and this is how I will measure my life." It is not easy to turn down opportunities that look good on paper but feel wrong in your gut. The alternative, which involves chasing a version of success that does not align with who you are, is far more costly. You may find yourself settling for a life that feels performative in a role you play rather than a purpose you live.

Cybersecurity taught me that success is often invisible. The best work in this field is the work no one notices. It is the vulnerabilities that do not become breaches, the systems that function without failure, and the trust that is quietly built with each safeguarded interaction. This kind of success does not come with applause or awards but is deeply meaningful. It is a reminder that success is not always about what the world sees. Sometimes, it is about the quiet assurance that you are making a difference.

To define success for yourself, you must let go of the idea that there is a right way to do it. You have to be willing to ask hard questions and sit with uncomfortable answers. What do I value most? What kind of life do I want to build? How can my work serve not just my ambitions but my purpose? These questions are not easy, but they are necessary. They are the foundation of a life that feels like your own.

True success is not static. It evolves as you do. The goals that feel urgent today may not matter tomorrow, which is okay. Authentic success is not about sticking to a plan. It is about staying true to yourself, even as your priorities shift. It is about finding fulfillment in the journey, not just the destination. And it is about understanding that your version of success is enough, no matter how different it looks from anyone else's.

Let this chapter serve as a reminder that success is not a standard to meet. It is a story you write for yourself, one choice at a time. You don't have to impress others; you only have to live in a way that feels honest, purposeful, and uniquely yours.

When we strip success of its borrowed expectations and define it on our own terms, we find something liberating. But I know the journey can feel isolating as if you are navigating uncharted waters without a map. That is where stories come in. They remind us that while success is deeply personal, it is also universal in its capacity to challenge, inspire, and teach. Every unique path serves as a mirror that reflects back what is possible when you refuse to settle for someone else's definition. I want us to look at stories of how others have redefined success for themselves and the lessons they leave behind.

Real-Life Examples of Redefining Success

When we think about meaningful success stories, we think of people who have challenged the script and broken away from society's ideals of what they should be. These people recognize that success is neither a monolith nor an assembly line where everyone has the same polished product. They inspire not because they are perfect but because they are undeniably authentic. To help you break the stereotypes of what success looks like, I find it imperative that we explore the stories of a few trailblazers who redefined success on their own terms so that you can get a new lens to view the limitless possibilities of what success can mean.

Fred Swaniker

Fred Swaniker is one of those people whose success story does not fit the typical mold; it is one of vision, courage, and unrelenting purpose. He grew up in Ghana and subsequently studied in the United States, where he had the opportunity to build a lucrative corporate career. As someone who has achieved it all, he could have gone about his days enjoying life as is, but instead, he saw a pressing leadership vacuum across Africa that couldn't be ignored. So, rather than focus on personal gains, he founded the African Leadership Academy and later the African Leadership University with a clear mission of nurturing a generation of ethical and entrepreneurial African leaders.

Swaniker's achievements and success aren't measured by titles or accolades but by the ripple impact of his work across Africa. Thousands of students have graduated from his institutions, and many are going on to solve critical challenges in their communities. And his story is a powerful reminder that success can be about creating opportunities for others to succeed instead of individual milestones alone.

Ngozi Okonjo-Iweala

If you want a masterclass in breaking the ceiling, there's no better story than that of Ngozi Okonjo-Iweala. As Nigeria's first female finance minister and later the director-general of the World Trade Organization, she shattered countless stereotypes about what leadership could look like despite her ascent not being without resistance. During her time in Nigeria's government, she implemented sweeping economic reforms in the face of vicious political opposition and never backed down once.

What I find particularly compelling about her journey isn't just the accolades but the global impact she has had. Her work redefines success beyond personal triumph, and this is evident in how she uses her platform to address systemic issues, such as tackling corruption and advocating for fairer global trade policies. Ngozi Okonjo-Iweala's work challenges us to see success as a tool for change, not just a reward for effort.

Trevor Noah

Born under apartheid in South Africa, Trevor Noah rose to global fame from circumstances that most would view as insurmountable. He was born to a Black mother and a white father, which meant his very existence was deemed illegal at the time. Still, Noah's experiences transformed into a superpower that propelled him to the very height of success. His memoir, *Born a Crime*, and his comedy are cultural touchstones that offer incisive commentary on race, identity, and resilience.

However, Noah's success is more about his capacity for telling globally resonant stories while staying rooted in his heritage rather than just his humor or ability to entertain. His path reminds us that success is not just about overcoming challenges but about using those challenges to create something that connects us all.

What do you think ties the stories of these brilliant Africans together?

It is neither the fields they represent nor the accolades they've earned. It is a fact that each of these individuals challenged external expectations and refused to let that define their trajectory in life. Fred Swaniker saw leadership as a collective effort, whereas Ngozi Okonjo-Iweala demonstrated that systemic change is a measure of true leadership, and Trevor Noah showed that even the most personal of struggles can become a bridge to shared understanding.

The lesson in each case is that success isn't a destination because these people had to align their talents and values with the impact they hoped to create. I want these stories to challenge you to rethink the metrics with which you currently measure achievements and remind you that the most powerful success stories are not just about the individual but about the broader legacy they leave behind.

Now, as you reflect on these real-life examples of success, take a moment to evaluate what success really means for you—do you want accolades and visibility, or do you want to make a quiet impact in your own corner of the world in a way that matters? Keep in mind that success is as diverse as the people who pursue it, and the beauty lies in its infinite potential for reinvention.

The stories of Swaniker, Okonjo-Iweala, and Noah should be powerful reminders that when viewed through the right lens, success is not just about personal wins but the connections you nurture and the value you create for others. And so, let me show you how redefining success includes embracing community and the lasting impact of shared purpose.

The Role of Community and Impact

Society often portrays success as a solitary pursuit, with a lone individual scaling a mountain to plant their flag at the summit. Still, the reality is far more communal and interconnected. There's not a single person in the history of the world who has succeeded in isolation, and the most enduring achievements are those that ripple outward to affect lives beyond our own. The point I am making is that community and impact are the foundation of success, and as much as they are its byproducts,

This truth is profoundly revealing regarding cybersecurity, particularly because the field is ultimately about safeguarding people, which extends the impact of cybersecurity professionals far beyond individual contributions. This principle is just as applicable outside of the professional sphere.

Think of everyone who shaped your journey until this moment, whether it's the teachers who pointed out your potential, the friends who validated your accomplishments no matter how small, or the mentors who showed you the way when the path was unclear. These people all have contributions that are an irremovable part of your story, just as your impact will become part of the stories of those you help later in life.

Here is where I want to discuss Fred Swaniker's African Leadership Academy again. Yes, he had an extraordinary vision, but where would all that be without the ripple effect of that vision? That's where true power lies because every graduate student becomes a leader in their own right and carries the mission forward. Therein lies the essence of community-driven success—the ability to multiply itself and create a shared-purpose network that grows stronger with every contribution.

Contrary to what societal expectations may have you believe, impact isn't always grand or immediate. In many cases, we find it in the small, quiet actions that compound over time. For example, as a cybersecurity professional, you likely won't ever meet the people whose data you work so hard to protect, but your work inevitably creates a foundation of trust upon which relationships, businesses, and even governments thrive.

In the same manner, the conversations you have, the encouragement you offer, and the time you invest in other people won't always yield visible results. Nonetheless, they are acts of connection that tend to have the most profound, lasting effects. By tying success to impact, you can change how you view challenges and learn to transform setbacks into growth opportunities for yourself and those around you. Communities thrive when their members are willing to share lessons learned, offer support, and build together, and this collaborative spirit inadvertently turns individual victories into collective progress.

Perhaps the most powerful aspect of community-driven success is its ability to challenge and expand our vision. We learn to see the world through new perspectives when we engage with others, which, in turn, pushes us to think bigger and to consider needs and possibilities beyond our own. This is where impact becomes transformative because now, it is about what you inspire and enable others to achieve, not just what you achieve individually.

Community is an ecosystem of ideas, values, and efforts that intersect and amplify one another, and I find that Strive Masiyiwa's philanthropy exemplifies this. His contributions to education and healthcare across Africa are investments in a shared future rooted in the belief that lifting others is a measure of true success, and his work demonstrates that the greatest legacies are built not in isolation but in collaboration.

In this moment, consider the communities that have shaped you and the impact you want to leave behind. More importantly, start reframing your mindset to see success not as an endpoint or a solitary achievement but as a process of giving, receiving, and creating transcendental value beyond your individual story. The question is not whether you will make an impact but what kind of impact you want.

A New Paradigm for Success

You don't have to confine success to a single narrative or measure it by fleeting milestones as society compels you to. Instead, you can find it in the stories you craft, the people you nurture, and the impact you leave behind starting from now. To fully embrace this new paradigm, you must let go of rigid definitions just as I did so that you can step into the possibilities that arise when success is reimagined as both personal and collective.

I wanted us to explore stories that challenge the conventional throughout this chapter so that you can see how impact can be a measure of success, how success can emerge from the most unexpected circumstance, and how it thrives when it reflects our authentic selves. As you can see, the thread that runs through these stories isn't one of perfection or predictability. You must find the courage to ask, "What does success mean to me?" and the resolve to answer that question honestly.

It is difficult to make this paradigm shift because it involves unlearning dated ideas about success. You must look inward and connect with your values and priorities in ways that will undoubtedly feel unfamiliar. However, doing this will open the door to a kind of success that feels expansive rather than limiting, meaningful rather than superficial. This will empower you to pursue goals that align with who you are rather than who society expects you to be.

Once again, success for you on this journey doesn't have to be about checking boxes or following a prescribed path. It can be about building an incredible connection to yourself and the world around you. When you deeply personalize success, it becomes deeply impactful, so much so that it shapes others' lives in ways you may not even realize. You contribute to a legacy of impact and growth by creating value, nurturing community, or inspiring someone else to realize their potential.

In this new paradigm, you must also acknowledge the role of imperfection. Conventional success stories often gloss over the missteps, whereas true success embraces them. This paradigm recognizes setbacks as an integral part of the journey necessary to shape character and deepen perspective. Thus, failure doesn't diminish success; it enriches it.

I know what you're thinking right now. *Does this mean I have to abandon my ambition?* Well, I didn't, and you don't. The goal is to redirect it so that you aren't merely striving for what looks good on the surface and what feels right deep within you. Making this shift doesn't mean rejecting hard work; it means channeling that work into goals that resonate on a deeper level.

Success is a series of choices, with each building on the last. It is the sum of your impact, relationships, and willingness to stay true to your evolving vision. However, it is one thing to understand what redefining success entails and another actually to do it. You need more than introspection to bring your vision to life—you need action.

The journey from aspiration to achievement demands focus, perseverance, and a willingness to adapt. It is not about rushing blindly toward your goals but about moving with intention and clarity.

In the next chapter, I will show you how to accelerate this process by turning insights into action. For now, take a moment to reflect. What does success look like for you, and how will you redefine it on your own terms?

Accelerating Success: The Formula for Making an Impact

Key strategies for fast-tracking success and lasting impact in one's chosen field.

The general idea is to approach success steadily through careful planning and consistent effort, but what if I told you it is possible to shift gears and accelerate? And I'm not talking about working harder or faster for its own sake; I'm talking about leveraging the right strategies to close the gap between where you are and where you want to be. Even better, I am talking about moving with precision and purpose so that you can turn potential into progress and progress into tangible impact.

Our world today is one where strategy reigns supreme due to its fast-paced nature, which means the rules of success have changed. Working hard and being diligent used to be enough, but now, you must also be strategic, adaptable, and keenly aware of every tool and opportunity.

That is precisely how I found myself at the top of the cybersecurity echelon. I am always on top of strategies, whether identifying emerging trends, cultivating meaningful connections, or mastering the art of focus. The point of acceleration is to make smarter choices by extracting more value from the ones you already have, not just adding hours to the day.

Understanding timing is a critical part of acceleration, as moving too quickly without direction can lead to missteps while hesitating at critical moments can result in missed opportunities. Thus, you must balance speed and strategy because that is where the true art lies. People who can master this balance are not just successful; they become transformative and create an impact beyond their immediate goals.

You may have seen this principle at play in how certain industries evolve. For instance, in cybersecurity, the ability to anticipate trends and act decisively can mean the difference between solving a problem and falling behind. As such, the best professionals are not those who work tirelessly but those who are masters at thinking strategically and leveraging tools and insights to remain ahead of cyber threats. Their success holds its roots in acceleration through an acute awareness of how to turn effort into exponential outcomes.

Strategic acceleration is a universal tool that extends beyond any singular field. It applies in every facet of life, whether you're an artist, an entrepreneur, or a tech. The path lies in your ability to move deliberately and efficiently toward your goals. You don't have to rush; you just have to make every step count. When you focus on what truly drives results and cut through distractions, you can unlock a level of progress that feels both sustainable and exhilarating.

I have mastered the formula for accelerating success, from leveraging data to cultivating strategic networks and optimizing execution to embracing innovation. I want you to be able to do the same, so this chapter is all about providing actionable insights that can fast-track your journey. Don't think of these strategies as shortcuts—think of them as accelerators designed to help you move forward with clarity, confidence, and purpose. No matter your field, the principles of acceleration remain universal. Let's dive in, and you'll discover how to turn calculated action into lasting results.

Leveraging Data and Trends for Impact

We are in an age with a ceaseless flow of information, where success is for those who can sift through the noise and identify the stuff that really matters. Like most people, you probably think of data as a collection of numbers and facts. However, when you harness it effectively, data can offer insights into patterns, behaviors, and opportunities, changing how you approach your goals for the better. Conversely, trends are the pulse of the world around us, a dynamic relation of what's constantly shifting and evolving. Together, data and trends create the most powerful foundation for accelerating success, particularly in this field of cybersecurity.

Data alone is powerful enough to turn uncertainty into clarity. It's like navigating a dense forest without a map, making every step a gamble and a potential detour. However, when you have the right map (data), you can chart a course, anticipate obstacles, and reach your destination in a precise amount of time. I see this analogy play out daily in this field, with professionals analyzing vast amounts of data to identify threats, predict vulnerabilities, and design systems that can respond quickly. If you want to be proactive and separate yourself from those who react rather than anticipate, data is your best friend on this journey.

Now, the thing is, you need discernment to leverage data effectively since not all data is valuable, and not every trend is worth following. Your challenge lies in developing a filter that can distinguish between meaningful insights and worthless distractions. To do this, you, of course, need clarity. What are your goals? What questions need answering to achieve them? When you approach data with specific objectives in mind, you transform it from overwhelming to actionable.

You must learn to spot trends before they peak, another critical skill in fast-tracking success. Often, trends begin as whispers—subtle shifts that go unnoticed by most but reveal enormous potential to those paying attention. You can see what I mean when you consider the rise of cybersecurity to be one of the highest-paying fields today. Decades ago, it was a niche, backroom operation for technology enthusiasts. Today, it is central to global infrastructure, and those professionals who saw the potential early weren't just ahead of the curve; they helped shape the curve.

Individuals who adopt trends early based on data typically find themselves at the forefront of opportunity, and this requires more than sheer luck. You need curiosity, observation, and a willingness to experiment, a pattern we've seen repeatedly in the evolution of industries. Entrepreneurs who embraced e-commerce early disrupted traditional retail, and technologists who anticipated the shift to cloud computing redefined how businesses operate. This underscores the importance of spotting trends when they are emerging instead of when they become obvious to all.

How do you develop this ability?

First, you must stay informed by following industry publications, attending conferences, engaging with thought leaders in cybersecurity, etc. However, you mustn't stop there. It helps to dig deeper by asking yourself why a trend is gaining traction, what needs it addresses, and how it aligns with your goals. You need this level of critical engagement to convert trends from fleeting phenomena into actionable opportunities.

True acceleration happens at the intersection between data and trends. For me, I don't just try to know what is happening; I also try to understand why it matters and how I can act on it. I do this by balancing my intuition with analysis. I find the facts in data, but intuition guides me toward applying them correctly. My most impactful decisions have come from this interplay where logic and creativity meet.

Let's talk about the growing adoption of artificial intelligence in threat detection, for example. There is clear data that traditional methods of identifying vulnerabilities are increasingly ineffective against sophisticated attacks. However, the trend is also unmistakable: AI-driven solutions are becoming the industry standard, and only those who recognized this early have been able to position themselves as leaders who can drive innovation in the field.

In any industry, the ability to leverage data and trends can create exponential impact. The key is to remain analytical and proactive by constantly seeking ways to connect the dots between what is happening and what could be.

As essential as leveraging data and trends is, it's only one part of the equation. You cannot achieve transcendental success in isolation, especially as it stems from relationships that unlock opportunities, spark innovation, and amplify impact. So, the next phase in accelerating success is establishing the power of a strategic network and how the right connections can propel you further and faster.

Building Strategic Networks

Behind every great achievement lies a network of relationships, including mentors sharing their wisdom, peers offering collaboration, and allies challenging your perspective. Strategic networks rarely occur in a vacuum—they are indispensable assets in today's hive-like world; the right relationships can open doors, expand opportunities, and provide critical insights to navigate challenges.

Many people think the key to building such a highly profitable network is to collect contacts or expand their LinkedIn following, but it is much more than that. A key part of the process is fostering meaningful connections aligned with your goals and values. The strength of a network is in its depth, which is about quality, not quantity. You must surround yourself with individuals who inspire, challenge, and empower you.

A strategic network is a support system that offers access to knowledge, resources, and opportunities otherwise out of reach. It's akin to an evolving ecosystem where every connection adds value, leading to a dynamic flow of insights and collaboration. A mentor might refine your skills, while a peer might introduce a pivotal opportunity. Combined, these relationships build a foundation for growth that exceeds individual efforts.

Success in cybersecurity often hinges on collaboration, as a strong network amplifies individual achievements, which means it's not just what you know but who you know—and how you leverage those connections to drive meaningful changes.

To build a strategic network, you need intention. Attending events or sending connection requests on social media isn't enough. Your goal is establishing genuine and mutually beneficial relationships, beginning with identifying the people you want in your network.

I want you to remember that authenticity matters when reaching out to potential professional network members. You don't have to impress people; you just have to be real with them by clearly articulating your intentions and what you offer. Trust me, I have made lasting impressions on many prospects with a thoughtful, sincere message. For example, when someone's work inspires me, I explain specifically what resonates and why.

I will admit that, like many, I made the common mistake of treating networking as transactional early in my journey. However, I've learned that professional networks thrive on mutual value exchange. You must contribute as much as you gain within your network because reciprocity is the key to enduring relationships where all parties feel valued and invested in mutual growth.

Once you've built a high-quality network, you will find that it fuels innovation because collaboration between diverse perspectives generates new ideas and solutions. No matter the industry, engaging with people who think differently challenges assumptions and inspires creativity, which pushes boundaries to achieve more.

To build your own strategic network:

- Assess your current network and identify gaps.
- Seek opportunities to engage with your industry's thought leaders, peers, and collaborators.
- Focus on adding value to every connection through sharing

insights, providing support, or maintaining regular contact.

Strategic networking involves constructing a foundation for sustained growth and influence. When approached with purpose and authenticity, your network becomes a vital asset—a source of strength, knowledge, and opportunities that accelerate your path to success.

Now, here's where focus and execution come into play. The difference between potential and progress is the ability to prioritize, cut through distractions, and turn plans into results. You can fast-track your road to success with these two skills, and I'll show you how I made it happen for myself.

Mastering Focus and Execution

The modern world is bursting with opportunities, yet distractions constantly pull us in countless directions. I've been there, juggling multiple responsibilities while trying to make sense of what truly deserved my time and energy. I've learned that success belongs to those who can block out the noise and channel their focus toward what truly matters. Focus and execution are deliberate disciplines that transform ambitions into measurable results.

I have learned from experience that focus is the backbone of successful execution. I cannot tell you how often I've had ambitious plans derailed simply because my attention was scattered across too many tasks. It's like trying to light a fire with the sun's rays but never holding the magnifying glass steady. When you channel your attention intentionally, you amplify your efforts, whereas divided attention drains your energy and delivers minimal impact.

To achieve focus, I had to retrain my mind to recognize what was worthy of my time and what wasn't. I sought out those things that truly deserved my attention, which required taking a long, hard look at my priorities. High achievers excel because they choose, deliberately, what not to do instead of doing everything. In a sense, mastering focus is a profound act of self-respect.

The Eisenhower Matrix is one of the tools I used to reshape how I managed my focus completely. It is a framework that categorizes tasks into urgent and important, important but not urgent, urgent but unimportant, and neither. A connection taught me to use this framework to pinpoint high-impact tasks and avoid distractions that drained my energy while contributing little to my goals. Of course, it was a game-changer.

Another strategy I stumbled across was the Pareto Principle, which I lean heavily on. Also called the 80/20 rule, it is the concept that 80 percent of results often come from 20 percent of efforts, and it has helped me zero in on what truly matters. I have applied this principle across my personal and professional goals by narrowing my efforts to the tasks that mattered most, which has helped me make smarter decisions and achieve greater outcomes.

Most importantly, I learned that ambitious objectives can feel overwhelming, but they offer much more clarity when I break them down into smaller, actionable goals. Every completed milestone boosted my confidence so much that it kept me moving forward.

Let's talk about creating results from plans. Execution is where ideas meet reality, and I've learned that even the best-laid plans mean little if they are not acted upon. So, I mastered the art of allocating specific time slots to focus on my work, which we call time-blocking. Through this, I established a structure that eliminated distractions and brilliantly enhanced my productivity. Knowing I had a dedicated block for a specific task allowed me to dive deeper into my work without constantly switching gears.

I also find task batching invaluable in execution. This involves grouping similar activities, such as responding to emails or tackling administrative work, to reduce the mental strain of jumping between unrelated tasks. It is an excellent way to free up mental space for creative problem-solving, often requiring uninterrupted focus.

Procrastination, I'll admit, was a challenge. The fear of failure or imperfection sometimes held me back, but I countered this by reframing tasks in my mind. I began to see them as opportunities to learn, improve, or create something meaningful instead of burdens. That was a powerful mindset shift that turned hesitation into action.

Along the path to mastering focus and execution, a very hard lesson I learned early in my career was balancing speed and precision. In the past, I used to feel pressured to act quickly, which compelled me to rush, leading to mistakes. On the other hand, I would also overanalyze and delay decisions, which kept me stuck. Eventually, I saw that achieving a balance between both sides was critical, so I taught myself to recognize when to accelerate and pause, as this is a hallmark of effective execution.

I'll never forget a project I worked on early in my journey. It involved developing a framework for a team, but I spread myself too thin trying to perfect every detail. This made me lose sight of the project's essence. Thankfully, the breakthrough came when I focused on one standout feature and poured my energy into refining it instead of chasing perfection in every area. That focus helped me to accelerate the timeline, and I delivered a product that the team truly appreciated. So, I was hoping you could embrace the principle of focusing, prioritizing, and executing your personal and professional goals.

Regardless of how much work you put into mastering the art of focus, you may find that it isn't enough to conquer the distractions of the modern world. It's important to amplify your efforts with the right tools and technology as a force multiplier. With technology and innovation, you really can elevate this journey and transform how you work to unlock possibilities that were once out of reach.

Before, technology used to be a mere accessory to ambition. It is a force multiplier constantly reshaping how we work, connect, and solve problems. Those who use it strategically can push the boundaries of what we once thought possible, which empowers them to create tangible outcomes out of aspirations.

As soon as I started on this path, I immediately realized that embracing tech and innovation was necessary for career advancement. The brother from church was one of the first to show me how the right tools could amplify my efforts, streamline my processes, and open up opportunities I couldn't access otherwise. I also learned that a tool, no matter how advanced, is only as effective as the vision guiding its use and that success with technology demands strategic application.

Technology extends human potential by enabling faster and more precise actions. However, acceleration isn't adopting every shiny new tool. You must identify technologies that align with your specific goals and integrate them thoughtfully into your plan. I have seen poorly implemented systems create bottlenecks that slow down progress rather than enhance it. You cannot overstate the importance of choosing tools that fit seamlessly into your objectives and workflows.

Innovation as a Driver

While technology provides the tools, innovation is the engine that drives progress. Innovation is not limited to groundbreaking inventions or disruptive startups. It includes rethinking approaches, refining processes, and embracing creative solutions to everyday challenges.

An excellent example is the rise of remote work technologies. Before they became mainstream, a few forward-thinkers saw the potential of tools like video conferencing and cloud collaboration to revolutionize workspaces. This gave early adopters a significant advantage in adapting seamlessly when the world suddenly shifted. This is the essence of innovation: the ability to see the potential before it becomes obvious and to act on it decisively.

Cultivating an innovative mindset requires curiosity and a willingness to experiment because innovation thrives on challenging norms and testing new ideas, even at the risk of failure. At the same time, you must learn something invaluable from each failure or mistake so that you can refine your approach and build solutions that truly make a difference.

Here are some strategies I have used to make technology and innovation work for me:

- **Stay Informed:** Regularly update yourself on emerging tools and trends. Industry publications, webinars, and conversations with thought leaders can help you stay ahead.

- **Start Small:** Before committing to new technology, test it on a smaller scale to evaluate its effectiveness. This reduces risk and ensures you invest only in solutions that prove their value.

- **Ensure Integration:** Choose tools that complement your existing systems and workflows, minimizing friction. A well-integrated tool enhances efficiency rather than adding complexity.

- **Automate Wisely:** Use automation to handle repetitive tasks, freeing up your time for strategic initiatives. Automation is not about replacing effort but redirecting it toward more meaningful work.

- **Invest in Training:** Even the most advanced technology is ineffective without user expertise. Equip yourself and your team with the skills to maximize the potential of new tools.

Keep in mind that no matter how advanced technology becomes, it cannot replace human insight that comes from creativity, critical thinking, and judgment. The most impactful innovations do not aim to replace human potential—they enhance it. As you integrate technology into your strategies, remember that its greatest power lies in complementing your unique perspective and expertise.

Acceleration is the result of deliberate decisions executed with clarity and purpose. The strategies we've covered in this chapter illustrate how momentum is built through alignment: understanding what drives progress and using that knowledge to move forward with confidence. Data sharpens your insights, networks broaden your reach, focus ensures precision, and technology amplifies your results. Success comes from weaving these elements together to create a path that reflects your goals and values.

This process is not rigid or one-size-fits-all. It evolves as you evolve, adapting to your unique circumstances and aspirations. The tools and approaches may change, but the principle is that acceleration requires intention. It's about consistently making choices that move you closer to the impact you want to create. This chapter has given you the framework—how you implement it is up to you.

ExcelMind: Your Bridge to a New Career

How the author's venture, ExcelMind, provides tools to help others on their journey to success. The role of mentorship and guidance.

Starting a new career is never easy. It's not just the skills you have to learn or the credentials you think you need. There's also the mental hurdle of believing it's even possible. Cybersecurity, for many, feels like an exclusive club with a high barrier to entry. People imagine it's reserved for computer scientists or IT professionals, leaving others to wonder if they'll ever find their place in this fast-growing field.

But as you now know, the gap isn't as wide as it seems, and the skills you need to thrive in cybersecurity are not out of reach. This is the premise on which **ExcelMind** was built: the idea that anyone, regardless of their background, can transition into this lucrative and rewarding field with the right guidance and tools.

ExcelMind is more than a program. It is a system designed to eliminate the guesswork and uncertainty of starting a cybersecurity career. This has little to do with abstract theories or endless certifications and everything to do with real-world training, practical strategies, and personalized support to ensure you don't just land a job but build a career with long-term impact.

This chapter is your introduction to ExcelMind and the vision behind it. It's for anyone who has ever doubted their ability to break into a new industry and feels stuck on the outside looking in. When you finish this chapter, you'll see why ExcelMind is the right tool for career growth and a bridge to a future you might not have thought possible.

The Vision Behind ExcelMind

I didn't come up with the idea of building ExcelMind overnight. It was born out of my journey and the obstacles I faced. As you know, I was working low-wage jobs without any technical background when my brother from church first introduced me to the the idea of pursuing a cybersecurity career. It seemed like an insurmountable challenge at the time, but with determination, I could create a better life that outweighed my doubts. I discovered a path forward through persistence and resourcefulness—a path I knew others could follow if they had the right guidance.

In my early days, I saw the barriers that kept so many talented people from breaking into the industry—expensive boot camps that promised the world but left participants burdened with debt and lacking the skills employers actually sought and degree programs that stretched on for years with little focus on the practical knowledge needed to excel in a rapidly changing field. Add those to the pervasive myth that cybersecurity was reserved for an elite group of tech geniuses, which meant those with no formal background felt like there was no way in.

These experiences shaped my vision for ExcelMind. I wanted to create something entirely different that dismantled these barriers and made cybersecurity accessible to anyone willing to put in the effort. My vision of ExcelMind is that it would act as a structured pathway to guide individuals like you from uncertainty to confidence and equip you with the tools and knowledge necessary to succeed. The program meets you where you are, whether you're just starting out or pivoting from an entirely different career.

Practicality is also an integral part of my vision for ExcelMind. I don't want you to be overwhelmed by abstract theories like when I first started, which is why this program focuses on real-world applications. You will learn skills immediately valuable to employers through hands-on training that mirrors the challenges you'll face on the job.

This goes beyond technical skills as ExcelMind offers support for resume building, interview preparation, career development, and many more things that will set the foundation for you to land your first job and build a successful career in cybersecurity.

The vision for ExcelMind is simple: to democratize access to one of the most in-demand fields of our time. I want everyone to see for themselves that cybersecurity isn't reserved for a select few; it is an opportunity for anyone ready to seize it.

My ultimate goal is for ExcelMind to become a testament to what's possible when determination is paired with the right resources.

But what really sets ExcelMind apart isn't just the vision or purpose. It is how we have brought those two things to life in its design, built to meet real-world challenges with practical, tailored solutions.

Unfortunately, the world of career development is filled with promises, but few programs truly deliver. ExcelMind is different. Because the focus is on creating results, not just teaching theories, my program can help participants close the gap between ambition and action by equipping them with all the right tools to succeed in a competitive field.

Let me show you what makes this brilliant program stand out and what makes it a game-changer for anyone looking to transition into cybersecurity.

What Makes ExcelMind Unique

As a learner, you bring your own unique story, and we've designed ExcelMind to honor that. Being the founder, I know that you don't need a uniform background or a predetermined skill set to become successful in the field of cybersecurity. Thus, whether you are starting fresh or pivoting from another profession, ExcelMind provides a learning experience tailored to your needs.

If you're a participant without any prior technical experience, there are foundational lessons to help you build that initial confidence. We can accelerate your growth through real-world applications if you have already been exposed to this field. Regardless of your background, the goal is to empower you to succeed on your terms, not mold you into a one-size-fits-all model with other participants. This is my way of ensuring we leave no one behind on this journey.

Additionally, this field requires learning to solve problems in real time instead of relying on theoretical knowledge. That is why we've integrated hands-on training into every step of the program so that you can engage in practical exercises and simulations that mirror the actual challenges solved every day by cybersecurity professionals. These scenarios will help sharpen your problem-solving skills and enhance your ability to think critically under pressure.

This emphasis on doing, rather than just learning, ensures that participants leave the program prepared to meet the demands of the field. We help build your confidence not only through instructions but experience as well. I am confident that by completing the program, you will be ready to step into a new cybersecurity role with resounding clarity and self-assurance.

I know how traditional degree programs can stretch on for years and years, and in the end, you have little to show except a mountain of debt. That is why I have chosen to take a different approach with ExcelMind, which is adopting an accelerated curriculum that focuses on efficiency without sacrificing depth. Within 90 days, you will have all the core competencies necessary to start earning six figures in cybersecurity.

I take this approach because I respect the time and resources of learners as I have been in similar shoes, meaning I know precisely where it hurts and how. With ExcelMind, you have a streamlined path to success with a focus on high-impact skills and eliminating unnecessary, redundant content. I'm not just promising you speed; I am promising you speed delivered through thoughtful design and targeted instruction.

From experience, people's favorite thing about ExcelMind is that the support doesn't end in the classroom or when the lessons end. No, this program is much more valuable than that. There is comprehensive support throughout every step of your career transition, from crafting standout resumes to mastering interview strategies. ExcelMind will provide all the guidance you need to secure opportunities in the cybersecurity field.

More than that, the program ensures long-term success by encouraging you to see beyond your first job and plan for sustainable growth in the industry. With mentorship, resources, and career coaching, be assured that you will remain competitive and adaptable as the field evolves.

Finally, the cost of entering cybersecurity often feels prohibitive for many since boot camps and degree programs often demand tens of thousands of dollars, which makes them inaccessible to most. I am changing this narrative through ExcelMind by offering high-quality training at an affordable price—you will be pleasantly surprised. Remember, the vision is to democratize access to cybersecurity education and break down barriers that have long excluded talented individuals like you.

If you're thinking, "Oh, but I'm not even in America," don't worry because I've got you. We designed this program with flexibility in mind. Therefore, participants can learn from anywhere in the world, meaning they can pursue their goals without uprooting their lives. This global accessibility ensures that ExcelMind can be your bridge to a new career no matter where you are.

We often think of learning as a linear journey—step-by-step, predictable, and confined to the walls of a classroom. However, real-world success requires a dynamic and experiential approach that is deeply connected to the realities of the field you are entering. This underpinning philosophy for ExcelMind shapes it into a program designed to teach and transform lives.

This philosophy—hands-on, accessible, adaptable, and community-driven—makes ExcelMind a life-changing learning experience that prepares participants for their first cybersecurity job and the dynamic, evolving career that follows.

The Future of Cybersecurity Careers

When you think about the future of cybersecurity, do you think about technology or people? The more the digital world's complexity increases, the more the demand for professionals capable of protecting it expands beyond traditional technical roles. This is evident in the evolution of cybersecurity, especially as it shifts toward inclusivity and opens up more opportunities for people with diverse skills and backgrounds. As such, the future of cybersecurity lies in creative problem-solving, strategic thinking, and the ability to adapt to an ever-changing technical environment.

Contrary to popular belief, many of the most critical roles in the industry require skills beyond technical knowledge, such as **Governance, Risk, and Compliance** (GRC), one of the prime examples. GRC professionals ensure organizations adhere to regulations and manage risks effectively through a blend of analytical capabilities and strategic insight.

Another area of cyber security is Security Awareness Training, which involves specialists educating employees on best practices for avoiding cyber threats. In this type of role, the field prioritizes communication and teaching skills, thus showcasing how cybersecurity increasingly relies on soft skills like empathy, clarity, ability to inspire behavioral change, etc.

Other roles that are becoming more essential include Incident Response Coordination and Cybersecurity Project Management, which mainly require organizational skills, leadership, and a deep understanding of processes to ensure swift, effective responses to cyber incidents.

As you can see, this diversity of roles signals a future where cybersecurity is accessible to everyone, regardless of professional backgrounds.

Furthermore, we are in a renewed age of Artificial Intelligence and automation, which are continuing to revolutionize industries, including cybersecurity.

Thanks to AI, machine learning systems now play a vital role in threat detection because they can analyze vast amounts of data and identify vulnerabilities faster than any human ever could. But don't get me wrong—this isn't saying human expertise will become obsolete. Rather, I am saying that the rise of AI places a critical emphasis on the importance of professionals who can interpret its findings, make informed decisions, and design systems that balance efficiency with ethical considerations. I believe the future of cybersecurity will see humans and technology working in tandem. For instance, automated tools will handle repetitive tasks, while professionals will focus on creative problem-solving, strategic planning, and responding to emerging threats.

Despite its unprecedented growth, the cybersecurity industry faces a significant talent shortage, with millions of unfilled positions worldwide and organizations struggling to find candidates who meet their needs. This presents both a challenge and an opportunity, and that is part of why I have built ExcelMind to close this divide.

The future of cybersecurity will depend on accessible education and training programs that democratize entry into the field. This means creating pathways for individuals without traditional technical backgrounds and focusing on building practical, job-ready skills. The more inclusive cybersecurity becomes, the stronger and more innovative the industry.

Personally, I consider the constant evolution due to the emergence of new threats daily as one of the most exciting aspects of cybersecurity because it enables us to push the boundaries of what is possible and stay agile and informed. Such an ever-evolving environment means that a career in cybersecurity is never stagnant. There will always be endless opportunities, from developing policies to designing advanced defensive systems, as long as cyberspace exists.

As you think about entering the field today, remember that the future holds job security and the chance to make a meaningful impact. As a cybersecurity professional, you'll be a guardian of the digital age, protecting everything from personal data to critical infrastructure. I know that this responsibility will offer you a deep sense of purpose and fulfillment.

As bright as the future of cybersecurity careers is, it is also competitive. It'll not be easy to achieve success without a commitment to continuous learning and the ability to adapt to new technologies and methodologies. Programs like ExcelMind are designed to prepare you for this reality. As you consider your own path, remember that any one skill or role does not define cybersecurity. It is a field that welcomes diverse perspectives, values adaptability, and rewards those willing to leap.

The future of cybersecurity is yours to shape—what part will you play?

In this chapter, I have shown you how ExcelMind's innovative approach meets the unique challenges of breaking into a competitive industry through its dynamic, adaptable framework that meets you at your starting point and empowers you to excel. With ExcelMind, you can have a roadmap prioritizing practical results.

Success begins with action. Take ExcelMind as an invitation to reimagine your future and take the first step toward a fulfilling career. The journey may not always be easy, but it is always worth it with the right guidance.

Now, let us explore the next part of your professional arsenal: **Lightforth**, the groundbreaking platform that harnesses the power of artificial intelligence to help you stay ahead in your career. From amplifying productivity to uncovering new opportunities, Lightforth builds on innovation to keep you at the forefront of an ever-evolving professional space. Let me show you how it can shape the next phase of your journey.

Lightforth: Harnessing The Power of AI for Career Advancement

An overview of Lightforth and how technology and AI-driven tools can accelerate personal and professional growth.

Creating Lightforth was personal for me. I know firsthand the frustrations of navigating a job search, especially when transitioning into a new field. Crafting resumes, applying to roles, and fighting the doubt and uncertainty that creep in with every rejection or unanswered application makes it a tedious process. The traditional job search process often feels like a full-time job on its own, almost as if designed to exhaust rather than empower. I wanted to change that.

You'll recall that I talked about how challenging it was to stand out when I first pivoted into cybersecurity and started applying for roles. It felt like my applications were constantly disappearing into a void because Applicant Tracking Systems would reject resumes before they ever reached human eyes. Interviews, when they came, were nerve-wracking because I didn't know how to prepare for the specific, technical questions recruiters would ask. These and many other experiences made me question whether I was on the right path, and I know I am not alone in that experience.

This is why I built Lightforth. I wanted to create a platform that takes the guesswork and inefficiencies out of job searching, something I wish I had during my own journey.

Lightforth is a tool for people who feel stuck. It provides much-needed clarity and direction in a process that often feels overwhelming. Combining the power of artificial intelligence with a human-centered design, this platform provides users with the resources they need to navigate the job-seeking process confidently.

This platform offers those exploring different careers an edge through the smart resume builder that aligns your experience with the specific demands of your preferred industry. Its automated application system ensures you do not waste valuable time on roles that are out of reach, while its interview preparation tools help you present yourself as a capable and informed candidate. These features are based on the challenges I faced and overcame, and I have now repackaged them into solutions anyone can use.

Don't think of Lightforth as another job search platform because it is more than that. It is a highly strategic tool designed to redefine how people approach career advancement. Every feature is built with intention, which is evident in how we focus on removing inefficiencies and empowering users to take control of their professional journey.

Here are some of the platform's core features and how they come together to create a seamless and effective career advancement solution.

The Smart Resume Builder

A resume is often the first point of contact between a job seeker and an employer. Yet, in today's job market, a well-written resume is not enough. Applicant Tracking Systems (ATS) act as gatekeepers, screening resumes for specific keywords and formats before reaching a recruiter's desk. This is where Lightforth's smart resume builder comes in.

Unlike generic resume tools, Lightforth's builder is optimized for ATS compatibility with the ability to analyze industry-specific requirements and create modern, visually appealing resumes in alignment with hiring trends. The templates are attractive and strategic, ensuring the content highlights skills and accomplishments that resonate with employers. Regardless of your background or experience, the resume builder adapts to your career stage through customization options that make your application stand out.

This feature is invaluable for anyone looking to become a cybersecurity professional. We've established that roles in this industry often come with technical prerequisites, so the good news is that Lightforth can ensure your experience is framed in a way that speaks directly to these demands. This will position you as a strong candidate from the moment your application is submitted.

Automated Job Applications

You obviously don't need me to reiterate how exhausting and time-consuming the traditional application process can be. We've all dealt with it at some point in our professional lives. From manually tailoring resumes to filling out forms and navigating company-specific portals, the entire process can feel like an endless chore, leaving job seekers burned out before they even get a response. Lightforth revolutionizes this process with its automated job application feature.

On the platform, you can set your preferences—such as desired roles, locations, and industries—and then leave Lightforth to do the heavy task of applying to hundreds, even thousands, of roles on your behalf each month. What better way to ensure your profile reaches as many opportunities as possible? Even better, this automation does not compromise quality. Every application is tailored based on your resume and the specific requirements of each role.

Once again, this feature will be a game changer for you when transitioning into cybersecurity since roles are often scattered across niche platforms or internal company systems, making them difficult to track. Because Lightforth centralizes this process, it can connect you with opportunities that fit perfectly with your skill set and career goals. It eliminates the guesswork so that you can focus on preparing for interviews and building your knowledge base.

Interview Preparation Tools

Needless to say, the job search doesn't end with an application. Interviews are often the most daunting part of the process, especially for roles that require technical expertise or field-specific knowledge. Lightforth's interview preparation tools are designed to alleviate this pressure and turn your anxiety into readiness.

The platform provides mock interview simulations tailored to the roles you are applying for, with simulations that go beyond generic questions to explore scenarios and challenges relevant to your chosen industry. For cybersecurity applicants, this means practicing for real-world questions about threat mitigation, risk assessment, and governance frameworks. The goal is to ensure you feel prepared, not just for the technical aspects but for articulating your experience and demonstrating your problem-solving skills.

Feedback from these mock interviews is immediate and actionable, and it includes highlighted areas for improvement and reinforcing your strengths. This feature helps build confidence, ensuring that you can present yourself as a capable, well-rounded candidate when facing a recruiter.

Personalized Insights and Analytics

One of Lightforth's standout features is its ability to provide personalized insights. I wanted us to add this particular feature because I have seen people go through the job-seeking process blindly, unsure of what is working and what is not. And I wanted Lightforth to change that by offering analytics on your applications, resumes, and overall strategy.

For example, the platform tracks how your resume performs with ATS systems and suggests improvement. It also monitors which industries and roles generate the most responses to help refine your approach. I know these are features that applicants will find particularly valuable due to the importance of aligning applications with specific skills and prerequisites.

Following this data-driven approach, you can make thoroughly informed decisions about your job search and, most importantly, concentrate your efforts where you are most likely to see results.

Accessibility and Scalability

We have built Lightforth to serve a diverse range of users, be it individuals just entering the workforce or professionals looking to pivot into new fields. Its accessibility is one of its greatest strengths. The platform is affordable compared to traditional job placement services or career coaching programs, thus breaking down financial barriers that often exclude talented individuals.

Moreover, Lightforth's scalability ensures it adapts to your needs as your career evolves. For cybersecurity professionals, this means staying connected with emerging opportunities, whether securing your first role or advancing to a leadership position. The platform's global reach also allows users to explore roles beyond their immediate geography, opening doors to remote positions and international markets.

Lightforth's capabilities go beyond streamlining processes—they redefine what it means to take control of your career. The real power lies in how these tools come together to empower individuals with diverse goals and experiences. Lightforth adapts to your journey and provides resources and a clear strategy for success.

How Lightforth Empowers Career Seekers

Job searching is deeply personal, and no two journeys are alike. For some, it is about building a foothold in an unfamiliar industry; for others, it is a strategic pivot or pursuing greater fulfillment. Lightforth stands out not because it provides tools but because it transforms those tools into solutions tailored to unique career paths.

When a person enters the job market for the first time, the most daunting challenge is often a lack of clarity. The endless advice, conflicting expectations, and complex application processes can overwhelm even the most determined candidates. We are countering this through Lightforth with a structured, straightforward approach that puts clarity at the forefront.

Instead of a single formula, you get a customized pathway that helps to identify your existing skills, even those you might not recognize as valuable at the moment. For example, an applicant with experience in retail management can be positioned as an excellent candidate for roles in fields where leadership, organization, and decision-making are essential. In essence, Lightforth teaches you to see opportunities you might not have considered ordinarily.

If you're a mid-career professional, you know the decision to change industries comes with a mix of ambition and anxiety. The fear of losing relevance or starting over can deter even the most confident individuals, but with Lightforth, you can reimagine these transitions and turn your past experiences into assets that drive future opportunities. We encourage users to view career pivots as strategic moves rather than detours, emphasizing the growing demand for hybrid skills.

We also show users how to reframe their resumes and interviews through storytelling. It is not about glossing over gaps but showing how diverse experiences create unique value. This perspective ensures that mid-career professionals do not just adapt to a new field but succeed within it.

Lightforth's power also lies in its ability to refine and amplify ambition for those already established in their careers. When you no longer chase entry-level positions, the challenge shifts to identifying roles aligning with long-term goals and personal growth. Lightforth's insights and analytics provide a strategic advantage to guide users toward opportunities suited to their expertise and aspirations.

Perhaps Lightforth's most transformative feature is its inclusivity, like ExcelMind. The platform's strength lies in serving individuals across all career stages, geographies, and industries.

Thanks to its leverage of automation, data insights, and global reach, Lightforth opens doors to opportunities that transcend traditional barriers, and the platform's adaptability ensures it meets users' needs at every turn. It levels the playing field, thus showing us that career advancement is not reserved for the few but accessible to anyone with the right tools and mindset.

Ultimately, Lightforth rejects the notion that career paths must follow a linear trajectory or fit a narrow mold. Instead, it celebrates the diversity of professional journeys and provides solutions that are as flexible and innovative as the individuals who use them.

With its combination of AI-driven insights, human-centered design, and a commitment to removing barriers, Lightforth is more than a platform—it is a movement. It empowers job seekers to think beyond limitations and approach their careers boldly and clearly, knowing that every step forward is backed by a system designed to support their success.

The Future of AI in Career Advancement

Artificial intelligence has shifted from being a futuristic concept to becoming an integral part of how industries and individuals operate. Its ability to process vast amounts of information, recognize patterns, and deliver insights at unprecedented speeds has redefined the rules of engagement for everything from healthcare to finance. The job market, long overdue for disruption, is no exception. AI is reshaping not only how people find jobs but also how they grow their careers.

At its best, the job search is about alignment—matching the right individual to the right opportunity. Yet, this process has historically been inefficient. Too often, resumes are rejected by algorithms that fail to capture the nuances of a candidate's qualifications. On the other end, employers struggle to find candidates who fit both their organizations' technical demands and cultural fabric. AI offers a way to reconcile both sides.

Lightforth uses artificial intelligence to make these connections smarter and more precise. It analyzes employers' needs and candidates' profiles to identify matches beyond surface-level keywords. For cybersecurity professionals, this means ensuring that skills like risk assessment or certifications in frameworks like ISO 27001 are highlighted in ways that resonate with hiring managers. Instead of leaving success to chance, Lightforth creates a system where talent meets opportunity with intention and clarity.

Additionally, the job market is shaped by shifting demands, emerging technologies, and unforeseen challenges. AI's real-time ability to interpret these patterns gives job seekers a significant advantage. Lightforth goes beyond simply pointing users toward open roles. It provides actionable insights that guide their career strategies.

For example, AI can identify industries experiencing rapid growth, like the increasing need for cybersecurity specialists to address vulnerabilities in AI-driven systems. It can also highlight skills that are becoming essential—helping users understand where to focus their learning efforts. Instead of merely reacting to market changes, Lightforth users can position themselves proactively, ensuring they are prepared for tomorrow's opportunities.

AI's role in career advancement is not limited to solving today's challenges. Its true potential lies in shaping the future. Imagine a platform that connects you to current opportunities and anticipates where your career could go based on emerging trends. Imagine tools that guide you through skills development, pairing real-time market data with personalized recommendations for growth. This is the vision Lightforth embodies.

Lightforth stands out in its philosophy that technology should enhance, not replace, human potential. AI is a powerful tool, but its value lies in its application. By leveraging AI to eliminate inefficiencies, provide insights, and foster growth, Lightforth creates a job search experience that is as empowering as it is effective. It is not just about finding a job but about building a career that aligns with your ambitions and abilities.

As AI continues to shape the future of work, platforms like Lightforth will lead the way in ensuring that individuals are not left behind but propelled forward. The next wave of career advancement will belong to those who embrace these tools with intention and purpose and see technology not as a replacement but as a partner in their success.

Lightforth is a cumulation of my lessons about aligning purpose with action. It embodies the belief that meaningful work comes from leveraging the right tools, adopting the right strategies, and remaining steadfast in pursuing growth. This vision didn't emerge overnight. It results from years of trial and error and invaluable insights gained through personal and professional challenges.

As we move into the next chapter, I'll share the key lessons that shaped my journey—lessons that guided not only the creation of Lightforth but also my approach to building a fulfilling and impactful career. Embrace these principles as guiding philosophies to chart your unique course toward crafting a legacy of profound impact.

Lessons Learned: Key Insights From My Journey

The most valuable lessons the author has learned throughout his journey and advice he would give to those following a similar path.

When I look back at my journey, it isn't to dwell on my past but to unearth the meaning behind every step I took. The setbacks, the triumphs, the doubts that lingered late into the night—each holds a story that reshaped how I approached life and work. Reflection, for me, is active and purposeful, a way of uncovering the lessons that have shaped my career and the paths of those I've had the privilege to guide.

Before, I used to think of success as something you reached or a finish line you crossed when all the conditions were perfect. But I've learned that success doesn't unfold in grand, cinematic moments. It builds slowly, shaped by choices you make when no one is watching and the grit it takes to keep going when the outcomes are uncertain. The journey itself becomes the real achievement, though you only understand that by looking back.

Although treated as a luxury by many, reflection is a tool anyone can use to break out of the noise of the moment and ask, "What mattered here? What did this teach me?" It's a way of cutting through the chaos, anchoring yourself purposefully, and seeing patterns you might have missed in the rush forward.

Over the years, I've sat across from people at different stages of their careers, each with their own versions of uncertainty. Whether they were stuck, pivoting, or chasing goals they couldn't yet articulate, one thing was clear: understanding the journey and truly processing it was the first step to moving forward.

Reflection turns what feels overwhelming into something you can work with. It reframes failure, clarifies values, and distills ambition into direction.

This chapter is about those realizations. The truths I've gathered aren't polished slogans; they result from real missteps, adjustments, and small victories. These lessons don't just sit on the surface—they run deep, granting clarity and practical wisdom for handling what's ahead. I hope they meet you where you are as answers so you can adapt to your own path.

As we move through these key insights, I encourage you to bring your own story into focus. Think about the moments that stretched you, the decisions that made you pause, and the values that remain constant despite everything else. Growth isn't just what you achieve; it's how you carry forward the lessons life has already given you.

Lesson 1: Growth is a Process, Not an Event

Growth isn't the dramatic, movie-like transformation we often imagine. It's not a lightning bolt of realization or a single breakthrough that changes everything overnight. In reality, it's a quiet, steady process that unfolds in the background of everyday life. It's built from small wins, deliberate choices, and countless moments when you decide to keep going, even when nothing changes.

I didn't always see it that way. Early in my journey, I believed results would mirror effort immediately. Work hard, and success will follow just as quickly—at least, that's what I thought. But life taught me a different lesson. Effort plants seeds; some sprout quickly, whereas others lie dormant, requiring patience and consistent care before showing signs of life. The real challenge is staying committed long enough to see the harvest.

Cybersecurity, the field where I eventually built my career, drove this lesson home. Breaking into a technical industry without a formal IT background was intimidating. At first, progress felt painfully slow because learning the basics took time, and preparing for certifications took effort. Plus, building confidence in an entirely new language of systems and protocols was harder than anticipated. But month after month, my small steps began to compound, and what once seemed overwhelming began to feel manageable. The process wasn't about sudden leaps forward. It was about stacking progress, one layer at a time, until the foundation was strong enough to support the next stage.

The hardest part of growth is its invisibility. At the moment, it feels like nothing is happening, and you need to refine your skills, revisit mistakes, and push through self-doubt. These actions feel small, even inconsequential, as you're doing them. But when you step back, the bigger picture comes into focus. Growth isn't something you measure in days or weeks. It takes months, years, or even decades. The person I was five years ago would hardly recognize the person I am today. That is the power of the process.

Growth is also unpredictable as it doesn't follow a straight line. Sometimes it's messy. Sometimes, it feels like you're moving backward. Those moments when progress feels paused are often the most important. Early in my career, I hit roadblocks that felt like failures. Looking back, I see them differently as recalibrations and opportunities to rethink my approach and realign my goals. I like to think of those moments as steps forward disguised in a different form.

This truth applies to anyone navigating change. Whether you're starting a new career, building a business, or reaching the next level in your field, the formula is the same. Growth requires consistency, even when it feels like nothing is happening. It demands trust in the process and the courage to move forward, even without guarantees. Sure, it isn't glamorous, but it is transformative.

So, how do you embrace growth as a process?

Start small. Let go of the need for instant results. Trust that every effort, no matter how small, contributes to the bigger picture. Take time to reflect on your progress. Those reflections can ground you when the future feels uncertain. Most importantly, allow yourself to grow at your own pace. Success isn't a race. It's a journey.

When I look back, the moments where I felt stuck or discouraged were lessons in disguise that taught me patience, resilience, and the value of showing up—even when the results weren't guaranteed. Growth isn't a single event. It's the sum of those moments, small and unremarkable on their own but extraordinary when seen together.

Lesson 2: Adaptability is a Superpower

Adaptability is the quiet resilience we often overlook. Louder qualities like ambition or determination overshadow it, but in a world driven by constant change, adaptability is what allows us to survive and, more importantly, thrive by giving us the capacity to recalibrate when circumstances shift, to find steadiness in uncertainty and to see challenges as doors to growth rather than walls blocking the way.

This truth has defined my journey. When I first arrived in the United States, the reality I faced was nothing like what I had envisioned. The professional foundation I had built no longer seemed relevant, and the opportunities I sought felt distant. I could have resisted and clung to the comfort of what I knew, but Instead, I leaned into the unknown, embracing unfamiliar roles and experiences—even humbling. That demanded a willingness to unlearn, relearn, and walk into spaces where I felt completely out of my depth.

Adaptability is not about ignoring fear or uncertainty. It is about moving forward despite them. The goal isn't to master everything at once but to push through the next step, the next challenge, and give me the grace to be a beginner without letting that define my future.

I didn't have this mindset inherently; I had to build it from scratch. Like most people, I craved stability, and change felt like a threat to that comfort. But stability, I have learned, is often an illusion, especially in fields like cybersecurity, where change is the only constant. Threats evolve. Technology advances. Strategies that worked yesterday can become obsolete overnight. To succeed in this environment demands a mindset that not only accepts change but uses it as fuel for innovation and growth.

One of my most profound lessons is that adaptability is not an exclusive gift— anyone can develop this skill. The first step is changing how we view change itself. For instance, instead of seeing it as a disruption, we can see it as a force for growth. Change is a natural challenge to our complacency that pushes us into spaces where we can stretch and evolve.

Building adaptability starts with curiosity. When faced with a challenge, ask yourself not, "Why is this happening to me?" but, "What can I learn from this?" Curiosity transforms fear into exploration and reveals possibilities you might otherwise miss. You can also nurture adaptability in yourself with small acts of flexibility in your everyday life. For instance, you might try a different problem-solving approach, seek fresh perspectives, and step outside your comfort zone in small but meaningful ways. These are habits that will, over time, strengthen your ability to adapt.

Adaptability also means letting go of rigid expectations because when we hold too tightly to how things "should" be, we miss out on how they *could* be. Some of the most rewarding moments in my career came from opportunities I had not planned for, which only became visible when I stopped clinging to a predetermined path. In cybersecurity, this meant saying yes to learning experiences and roles that did not fit my original vision but ultimately laid the groundwork for success.

It is important to understand that adaptability does not mean compromising on everything. It is about balance. Remain flexible while staying rooted in your purpose. Picture a tree in a storm. Its branches bend with the wind, but its roots stay anchored.

Adaptability allows us to adjust to challenges without losing sight of what keeps us grounded.

In both life and work, adaptability drives growth that transforms setbacks into opportunities, uncertainty into possibility, and challenges into stepping stones for something greater. The world will not pause for us to catch up. It rewards those who move with it, adapting, innovating, and growing through change.

Looking back, I realize that adaptability shaped who I am and gave me the courage to embrace the unknown, the tools to navigate transitions, and the perspective to recognize opportunities I never dreamed of. For anyone navigating a career shift, a life transition, or even just the uncertainty of today, adaptability is the superpower that will carry you through.

Lesson 3: Relationships Matter More Than You Think

The myth of the self-made individual is deeply ingrained in our culture. We admire the lone visionary, the one who defied the odds and carved a path entirely on their own. But the truth is, no one achieves anything meaningful in isolation. Behind every success story are relationships—connections that inspire, challenge, and amplify our efforts.

When I look back on my career, it's impossible to separate my achievements from the people who stood alongside me. Early in my journey, I underestimated the power of relationships. I thought success was a solo endeavor that required me to rely solely on my drive and determination. It didn't take long to realize how limiting that mindset was. The turning points in my career often came through people—mentors who offered guidance, colleagues who shared their insights, and networks that opened doors I couldn't have reached on my own.

Building meaningful relationships isn't about collecting contacts or amassing a long list of LinkedIn connections. It's about cultivating genuine connections rooted in mutual respect and shared goals. One of the most pivotal relationships in my career came during my transition into cybersecurity. Conversing with a mentor didn't just introduce me to the field but provided a way to maneuver it. That guidance saved me months, if not years, of uncertainty and missteps.

But relationships aren't just about receiving help. They're about giving it, too. Some of the most fulfilling moments in my career have been opportunities to pay it forward—to mentor others, share knowledge, and open doors for people just beginning their journeys. Helping others succeed doesn't diminish your own success; it amplifies it. In fact, these reciprocal connections create a ripple effect that extends far beyond what any one person could achieve alone.

The strength of a relationship lies in its authenticity. People are drawn to those who show up with sincerity, who listen more than they speak, and who prioritize long-term trust over short-term gain. When done right, networking isn't about what you can extract from someone. It's about building a foundation of respect and value that benefits both parties over time.

So, how do you cultivate relationships that truly matter? Start with curiosity. Take a genuine interest in the people you meet, not because of what they can do for you but because of who they are. Ask thoughtful questions, listen to their stories, and look for ways to add value to their lives. Small acts of kindness, like sharing resources or offering encouragement, build lasting goodwill.

Another critical component is consistency. Relationships don't thrive on sporadic effort. They require ongoing care, whether a quick check-in, a note of congratulations, or simply showing up when someone needs support. These small gestures reinforce trust and keep connections alive, even when life gets busy.

Finally, don't underestimate the power of vulnerability. Authentic relationships are built on honesty, not perfection. Sharing your struggles and being open about your journey invites others to do the same. Vulnerability fosters connection, reminding us that success isn't a straight line for anyone.

At its core, success is rarely about individual effort alone. It's the result of a formal or informal network of people who challenge, support, and uplift each other. Relationships matter not just because they open doors but because they make the journey more meaningful. They remind us that no matter how ambitious our goals are, we're not meant to achieve them alone.

As I reflect on my own path, the relationships I've built stand out as some of the most valuable investments I've ever made. They taught me lessons I couldn't have learned on my own, offered opportunities I wouldn't have found otherwise, and reminded me that true success is as much about connection as it is about achievement.

Lesson 4: Success Lies in the Details

We often celebrate the bold strokes of achievement: the visionaries, the game-changing ideas, the grand moments of triumph. Yet, what truly separates those who succeed from those who struggle is often not found in the sweeping gestures but in the details. The work behind the scenes, the willingness to refine and revisit, the deliberate attention to what others might overlook—is where success takes root.

Early in my career, I misunderstood this. I believed success came from ambitious goals and visionary thinking alone. But I soon realized that even the grandest plans falter if the groundwork is shaky. In the pursuit of growth, it wasn't the big decisions that tested me most; it was the discipline to focus on the small, essential elements of the process.

In cybersecurity, this truth becomes unavoidable. A single overlooked vulnerability can open the door to catastrophic breaches. The attention to configurations, the double-checking of protocols, and the consistent refinement of processes make systems secure. While this field taught me the importance of precision, the lesson extends far beyond technical domains. In any career or endeavor, details are the glue that holds everything together.

The challenge, of course, is that details demand patience and care in a world that prioritizes speed. The pressure to act quickly often comes at the expense of thoroughness, and while it might save time in the short term, the cost of rework or failure often outweighs any perceived gains. I've learned that slowing down, asking the right questions, and being intentional are not delays but investments.

This doesn't mean obsessing over every decision. Attention to detail is not about perfectionism, which can stifle creativity and progress, but about being deliberate and thoughtful. Understanding that even small adjustments can lead to disproportionately large results. In my career, I succeeded most when I committed to clarity, whether it was understanding the problem I was solving or ensuring my approach was sound.

The power of details lies in their cumulative impact. Consider the difference between a hastily assembled resume and one crafted with care, tailored to highlight strengths that align with the role. The latter speaks volumes about your seriousness and professionalism. The same applies to the way you present yourself in an interview, structure a business pitch, or lead a team meeting. It's not just the content that matters but how it is delivered.

I've found that attention to detail is often the mark of excellence. It signals not only competence but also respect for your craft, for others, and for the goals you are pursuing. Success rarely results from doing everything; it comes from doing the right things well. This focus requires the willingness to prioritize, to ask what truly matters, and to pour your energy into refining those aspects.

Looking back, the moments I regret most were not the ones where I failed outright but those where I allowed carelessness to undermine my potential. Rushing through tasks, skipping steps, or ignoring what seemed minor at the time often led to setbacks that could have been avoided. On the other hand, the moments that stand out as pivotal were those where I committed fully to the process, even when it felt tedious. In those moments, I learned the importance of treating even the smallest tasks with the same level of care I gave to the big ones.

Ultimately, success isn't about grand gestures or sweeping changes. It is built on the foundation of steady, thoughtful actions. You set yourself apart by embracing the details, not as a burden but as an opportunity. In every career, every endeavor, and every ambition, the details shape the outcome far more than we often realize.

Lesson 5: The Importance of Lifelong Learning

The world is changing at an unprecedented pace. Fields that once moved predictably now evolve rapidly, driven by technological breakthroughs, shifting societal expectations, and global events. In such a landscape, staying still is not an option. Lifelong learning is not just a competitive advantage but a survival skill.

When I began my transition into cybersecurity, I was struck by how quickly the field moved. New threats emerged daily, and the tools to combat them constantly evolved. What I learned early on was that mastery was a continuous process of growth and adaptation. The knowledge that brought success yesterday might no longer be enough tomorrow. This realization shaped my approach to my career and my entire mindset.

Lifelong learning starts with curiosity. It is the willingness to ask questions, to challenge what you think you know, and to explore new perspectives. This meant acknowledging that I didn't have all the answers and embracing that as a strength rather than a limitation. Curiosity drove me to learn about emerging technologies, seek out mentors who could guide me, and dive into books and courses that expanded my understanding of the field.

One of my most humbling lessons is that true growth requires humility. It is easy to feel overwhelmed or even defensive when faced with the need to learn something new, especially in the presence of those who seem more advanced. But humility allows you to step back, acknowledge where you have room to grow, and approach learning as a collaborative process. Some of my greatest breakthroughs came not from solitary study but from conversations with peers and mentors who challenged my assumptions and broadened my perspective.

Lifelong learning is not limited to formal education. In fact, some of the most impactful learning happens outside the classroom. It happens when you take on a project that forces you out of your comfort zone, read a book that challenges your worldview, or reflect on a failure and extract the lessons hidden within. Learning is a practice, not a destination. It is something you do, not something you complete.

In cybersecurity, the stakes of lifelong learning are particularly high. A professional who doesn't stay updated risks becoming obsolete in a field where yesterday's solutions may no longer work. But this principle applies to any career. The world rewards those who stay curious, adapt to change, and invest in their growth with the same rigor they apply to their work.

One of the most powerful strategies for lifelong learning is setting clear, actionable goals. Instead of vaguely aspiring to "learn more," identify specific areas you want to improve or explore. Maybe it's mastering a new technology, deepening your understanding of an industry trend, or developing a soft skill like communication. Breaking learning into tangible steps makes an abstract concept into a manageable process.

Another strategy is to embrace diverse learning formats. In today's world, education is more accessible than ever. Online courses, webinars, podcasts, and even social media platforms provide endless opportunities to acquire new knowledge. The key is not to overwhelm yourself but to choose resources that align with your goals and integrate them into your routine. Fifteen minutes spent listening to an insightful podcast during a commute can compound into significant growth over time.

The commitment to learning also fosters resilience. When you see challenges as opportunities to learn rather than threats to your competence, you become more adaptable and less afraid of failure. This mindset enhances your career and enriches your life, giving you the tools to navigate uncertainty confidently.

I can trace my success to moments when I embraced learning instead of resisting it. Each new skill, each fresh perspective, and each lesson learned added layers to my capabilities and opened doors I didn't know existed. Lifelong learning isn't just about staying relevant; it's about expanding what's possible.

The beauty of learning is that it never ends. No matter how much you know, there is always more to discover, more ways to grow, and more opportunities to create impact. The question is not whether you will learn but how intentionally you will approach it. In a world where change is constant, lifelong learning is the anchor that keeps you grounded while propelling you forward.

The lessons we embrace don't just shape our own paths; they inspire others and ripple outward in ways we can't always predict. Growth, integrity, and adaptability are catalysts for real, tangible change. As we reflect on these principles, we see their power not just in theory but in action.

In the next chapter, I want to share the stories of people who started where you might be right now—uncertain, searching for direction, and wondering if a better career was truly within reach. They didn't just take a leap; they followed a proven path. Through their dedication and the tools I provided, they transitioned into thriving cybersecurity roles, creating an impact for themselves and their families and communities.

These stories are about more than success; they're about possibility. Let their experiences inspire you to take that first step toward a career in cybersecurity. Because if they can do it, so can you.

Real Stories, Real Impact: Testimonials and Lessons from Others

This chapter shares stories and testimonials from people who have turned their lives around by following these principles. Their experiences will show the reader what's possible and motivate them to take action.

Success often feels like a distant dream until you see it realized in the lives of others. Something is grounding about hearing stories of real people—those who have struggled, persevered, and triumphed. These aren't tales of overnight success but of steady, deliberate effort. They show us what's possible when the right guidance meets unshakable determination.

When I started mentoring individuals who aspired to break into cybersecurity, I never imagined the profound transformations I'd witness. Many came to me at a crossroads in their lives—some financially strained, others burdened by unfulfilling jobs, and a few simply looking for purpose in their careers—a willingness to try connected them all, even when the odds seemed stacked against them.

In this chapter, you'll meet some of these remarkable individuals. Their backgrounds are as diverse as their challenges. Teachers, delivery drivers, recent graduates, and even professionals from unrelated fields took steps that seemed improbable at first. They were not tech experts or seasoned IT professionals, but their journeys into cybersecurity reshaped their futures.

Take Daniel, who faced rejection after rejection but refused to give up. When he enrolled, it was his last shot, and with a renewed resume and the skills he had gained, he landed interviews and secured a role that once felt unattainable.

Then there's Oluebube, whose persistence turned interviews into job offers. She walked into negotiations knowing her worth, refusing to settle for less than she deserved. She broke into the industry by applying the tools and strategies she learned, proving that preparation and self-confidence can be just as critical as technical skills.

These stories represent a growing movement of individuals who have defied traditional barriers. They remind us that cybersecurity is not reserved for those with decades of IT experience. It is an evolving field that values problem-solving, adaptability, and the courage to step outside your comfort zone.

What stands out in every story is the people's resilience behind it. They faced challenges head-on—whether it was balancing life's demands with rigorous training, settling down in an unfamiliar industry, or overcoming their own doubts. Each one shows that success isn't about perfection but persistence.

As you read these stories, think about your own journey. What obstacles are holding you back? What opportunities have you overlooked? These stories prove that transformation is possible, even in the face of doubt. They show that you can take control of your future with the right tools, guidance, and mindset.

These individuals didn't just land jobs. They are now creating their own impact, and their journeys demonstrate that success is about inspiring others and uplifting families. This chapter aims to show you what's possible when you decide to act. As you turn the page, let their stories remind you that your own life-changing opportunity could be closer than you think.

Yemi's Story

When Yemi first joined my program, he wasn't sure if cybersecurity was the right path for him. With a degree in sociology and a master's in human resources, he had built his career around people, not technology. Yet, something about transitioning into a new field resonated with him. He told me he wanted a career with growth, stability, and the chance to make a real impact.

From the moment we spoke, I could tell Yemi was serious about succeeding. He wasn't just looking for shortcuts; he wanted a clear, structured path. While cybersecurity might feel unfamiliar, I assured him his background gave him valuable transferable skills. I walked him through the program's framework, starting with foundational concepts and gradually building up to technical knowledge. Each module was designed to demystify the field, and Yemi immersed himself fully.

What impressed me most about Yemi was his discipline. He finished the modules in two weeks, an incredible pace, especially for someone without a tech background. But what made the difference was how he used the tools we provided. His resume, initially generic, became a powerful asset after going through LightResume. Together, we tailored it to highlight his compliance, problem-solving, and communication skills—qualities cybersecurity employers value.

Yemi also dedicated himself to mastering the interview process. He used our mock interview platform to practice technical questions and refine his answers to behavioral scenarios. I still remember one of our follow-ups where he shared how much more confident he felt after receiving feedback on his responses. Clearly, he wasn't just learning; he was applying those lessons in real time.

The job search was not without its challenges. Yemi sent out dozens of applications, faced rejections, and encountered silence from employers. Each time, he returned to me asking, "What can I do better?" It was his willingness to adjust and improve that set him apart.

Eventually, his efforts paid off. Yemi secured a role as a Security Analyst with a starting salary of $115,000. I could hear the pride in his voice when he called to tell me the news. This role allowed him to monitor and protect systems, ensuring the safety of sensitive information. For someone who had once doubted his ability to work in a technical field, he had proven to himself and others how capable he was.

When I reflect on Yemi's journey, what stands out is his dedication to the process. He trusted the program, worked tirelessly, and kept faith in his ability to succeed. His story reminds me why I do this work. It's not just about helping people get jobs. It's about helping them realize their potential, even when the path seems uncertain.

Daniel William's Story

When Daniel Williams joined the ExcelMindCyber program, I could sense his weight. He wasn't just bringing his aspirations—he was bringing the last ounce of his faith. Daniel was at a crossroads, with his savings nearly gone and rejection emails piling up. He told me that enrolling in the program felt like his final shot, a decision fueled more by desperation than confidence.

His journey was anything but smooth. Daniel had already faced a crushing blow when he failed an essential cybersecurity certification exam. To make matters worse, the certification body told him that retaking the test was not an option. The news devastated him. When we spoke about it, I remember his voice carried a heavy mix of disappointment and uncertainty. But even in that moment, he was willing to fight for a way forward.

The first step was to rebuild his confidence. My team worked closely with Daniel to update his resume and refine his LinkedIn profile. We crafted a professional narrative that highlighted his strengths and aligned with the roles he wanted to pursue. Daniel didn't just follow instructions—he leaned into the process, trusting that these small adjustments could lead to big results.

Then, something incredible happened. Daniel received an email from the certification body reversing their decision. They reinstated him and permitted him to reschedule his exam. I'll never forget the moment he called me to share the news. For him, this wasn't just about getting another chance—it was a validation of his faith and determination.

Shortly after, the tide continued to turn. A recruiter reached out, impressed by Daniel's updated resume and presence on LinkedIn. The recruiter told him, "Your resume stands out. I've shortlisted six candidates for this role, but yours caught my attention." That conversation led to an offer with a starting salary of $120,000. For someone who had spent months doubting his worth, this was more than a job—it was a lifeline.

Daniel's transformation wasn't just professional; it was deeply personal. I remember him saying, "The day I signed up, I cried. I told God this was my last shot, and He answered my prayer." His journey is a powerful reminder of what resilience, faith, and preparation can achieve.

For me, Daniel's story embodies what this program is about. It's not just about landing a job—it's about reigniting hope and showing people what they're truly capable of when given the right tools and guidance. His success continues to inspire me, and I hope it inspires you too.

Oluebube's Story

When Oluebube joined my program, she was stepping into unfamiliar territory. With no technical background, she was unsure if cybersecurity was the right fit. But what stood out about her was her willingness to embrace the challenge. She approached every step with determination, proving that success often begins with a bold decision.

From the start, I could see her potential. She trusted the process and leaned into the tools we provided. Together, we worked on crafting a standout professional identity. Her resume, initially vague, became a polished reflection of her transferable skills and potential. We wrote recommendation letters that spoke to her dedication and adaptability. Her LinkedIn profile was overhauled to showcase her readiness for a cybersecurity career. Oluebube actively engaged with every part of the process, ensuring nothing was overlooked.

Her diligence carried over to interviews. Initially daunting, the interview process became an opportunity for her to shine. She used mock interview sessions to practice articulating her skills and addressing gaps in her experience. She confidently negotiated when one company offered her a Compliance Analyst position at $94,000. "I believe my skills justify a higher offer," she told them. They agreed to raise the salary to $100,000.

The role was a perfect match for Oluebube. As a Compliance Analyst, her responsibilities included evaluating and enforcing security policies to meet regulatory standards. While the job initially felt unfamiliar, it didn't take long for her to excel. The problem-solving and critical thinking skills she had developed during her training became invaluable.

Reflecting on her journey, Oluebube often shares how preparation and persistence shaped her success. "I was nervous, but I had done my homework. When they accepted my terms, it felt like all the effort was worth it," she told me.

Her story proves that success in cybersecurity isn't limited to those with technical expertise. Employers valued her adaptability, communication skills, and eagerness to learn. These qualities, paired with her dedication, made her an ideal candidate.

For Oluebube, this new role wasn't just about financial stability. It marked the beginning of a career she never thought possible.

Her experience shows how stepping into the unknown can lead to opportunities beyond your imagination. It's a reminder that anyone can redefine their future with the right tools, guidance, and persistence.

Phoebe's Story

When Phoebe reached out to join my program, her motivation was clear: she wasn't just looking for a career change; she wanted to prove to herself that she could thrive in a field she had once considered out of reach. She brought a unique blend of skills from her background in human resources, but what stood out most was her determination to reimagine her potential.

Unlike many participants, Phoebe didn't see the technical aspects of cybersecurity as an obstacle. Instead, her initial struggle was recognizing how her existing skills could translate into this new world. "How does what I know fit into cybersecurity?" she asked me during our sessions. That question became the foundation of her transformation.

We began by analyzing her strengths. I pointed out how her experience managing policies and resolving conflicts in human resources directly related to the compliance and governance side of cybersecurity. She had a knack for understanding rules and ensuring people followed them—an invaluable skill in a field that demands precision and accountability.

Phoebe approached the training program with an open mind and an incredible work ethic. Despite balancing family responsibilities and a full schedule, she made time to engage deeply with the modules. Her ability to draw connections between the concepts she was learning and her past experiences gave her a distinct edge.

One moment I'll never forget was helping her prepare for an interview with a multinational organization. The role required a mix of leadership and technical knowledge, and Phoebe was determined to present herself as the ideal candidate. We focused on framing her human resources background as an asset during our mock interview sessions. She practiced explaining how her ability to manage people and policies aligned perfectly with the role's demands for governance and compliance.

The interview process was rigorous, but Phoebe's confidence grew with each step. She called me after her final round, thrilled to share that the interviewers had been impressed by her ability to articulate the connection between her previous work and their needs. Soon after, she received an offer for a Cybersecurity Governance Specialist position with a starting salary of $105,000.

For Phoebe, this wasn't just about securing a job—it was about stepping into a version of herself she had only dreamed of becoming. "I never thought cybersecurity was for someone like me," she told me, "but now I see how my unique perspective adds value."

Her story is a testament to the power of recognizing your potential and leveraging it in unexpected ways. It's a reminder that breaking into cybersecurity—or any new field—isn't about reinventing yourself. It's about building on what you already have and trusting that the right support can help you navigate uncharted territory.

A Q&A with the Author's Reflection

This chapter reflects on the power of persistence and preparation, as shown through the stories of individuals who have walked the cybersecurity path. While these experiences are deeply personal, they also point to universal truths about growth, resilience, and the importance of support. Here, I address the questions I often hear, drawing connections between these stories and their broader lessons.

Q: What motivated you to create ExcelMindCyber? It started with my own journey. When I transitioned into cybersecurity, I faced roadblocks at every turn. I didn't know which certifications to pursue or how to translate my background into something the industry would value. I had to figure it out through trial and error, often feeling isolated and uncertain. ExcelMindCyber was born out of my desire to give others what I didn't have—a clear roadmap, practical tools, and the confidence to believe they could succeed in this field.

Q: What challenges do most people face when entering cybersecurity? Many participants struggle with self-doubt, feeling that they don't have what it takes because they lack a technical background. This mindset can be the biggest obstacle. Cybersecurity isn't just about technical skills—it's about problem-solving, communication, and the ability to think critically under pressure. Another challenge is the overwhelming amount of information out there. Without a guide, it can be hard to know where to focus. That is why having structured support makes such a difference.

Q: How do the principles in this book connect to long-term success? The principles of preparation, persistence, and leveraging support are foundational. They are not just strategies for getting your first role; they are habits that sustain growth throughout a career. Cybersecurity evolves rapidly. The people who excel are the ones who commit to lifelong learning, stay adaptable, and build relationships within the field. The individuals in this chapter exemplify what happens when you approach challenges with these principles in mind.

Q: What is the one thing you hope readers take away from this chapter? If there is one lesson, it is that success is not reserved for a select few. It is achievable for anyone willing to put in the work and trust the process. The people featured here didn't have perfect paths. They faced setbacks and doubts, yet they kept going. Their stories show that progress is what matters, not perfection.

Q: How important is a community in achieving success? Community is essential. Many of the individuals in this chapter succeeded because they weren't alone. They had access to mentors, peers, and resources to guide them through the tough moments. Cybersecurity, like any field, thrives on collaboration. Building a supportive network is one of the smartest moves anyone can make, whether starting or already established.

Q: How do these stories connect to the mission of ExcelMindCyber? ExcelMindCyber is about more than landing jobs. It is about helping people see the potential within themselves. It equips participants with the skills and confidence to assume roles they might never have considered. The stories in this chapter prove that with the right tools and mindset, transformation is not only possible—it is inevitable.

The experiences shared in this chapter are not just inspiring but instructive. They show what happens when preparation meets opportunity and when individuals commit to growth, no matter how daunting the path may seem. But success is never isolated—it ripples outward, touching lives, families, and communities in ways that extend far beyond the individual. In the next section, we will explore this broader impact and the lasting legacy of those who dared to believe in their potential.

Giving Back: True Leadership nd Impact Beyond Success

Success means nothing if you don't lift others along the way. This chapter discusses the importance of community involvement, mentorship, and creating a legacy bigger than oneself. Giving back is the ultimate measure of success.

Success, at its core, carries a profound responsibility—a call to action to uplift, empower, and leave a legacy of positive change. Giving back has always been more than an obligation; it has been a cornerstone of my life's purpose. The journey to achieving professional excellence and building impactful initiatives has been deeply rewarding, but the most meaningful moments have come from the opportunities to touch lives and inspire transformation.

Through the Tolu Michael Foundation and various professional endeavors, I have been privileged to see firsthand how empowerment and guidance can ignite potential and create lasting impact. This chapter reflects on the broader mission of using success to foster meaningful change, celebrating the people and communities who have been part of this journey.

The idea for the Tolu Michael Foundation (TMF) was born out of a deep-seated desire to address the challenges I witnessed growing up in Nigeria. Poverty, lack of education, and systemic inequality were not just abstract issues—they were realities that shaped the lives of many people around me. As I navigated my career and experienced the transformative power of opportunities, I knew I wanted to create a platform to extend those opportunities to others.

TMF is more than a philanthropic endeavor. It is a mission-driven organization committed to eradicating poverty, creating sustainable job opportunities, and ensuring that economic empowerment is accessible to all. Since its inception, the foundation has awarded scholarships to thousands of students, provided financial aid to underserved communities, and organized outreach programs that address pressing social needs.

These initiatives are guided by a simple but powerful belief: by providing the right resources and support, we can create a ripple effect of positive change. A scholarship awarded to one student is not just an investment in their future but an investment in the family and community that benefit from their success.

One of the key pillars of TMF is empowerment. The foundation's Global Empowerment Program provides financial aid, grants, and scholarships to individuals with high potential and ambitious goals. To date, these initiatives have supported over 14,000 individuals worldwide, with more than $50,000 disbursed directly to aid them in achieving their dreams.

The focus of this program is not just on financial support but on equipping individuals with the skills and confidence to take control of their lives. Through training workshops, mentorship programs, and personalized guidance, TMF ensures that recipients are not just beneficiaries but active participants in their own growth.

A story that stands out is that of a young woman who received a TMF scholarship to complete her education. Her circumstances had made higher education seem unattainable, but with the foundation's support, she not only graduated with honors but also secured a job that allowed her to support her siblings and contribute to her community.

These moments remind me that empowerment is not about solving every problem for someone but about giving them the tools to solve problems for themselves and others.

TMF's commitment to education extends beyond traditional classrooms. Recognizing the growing importance of digital literacy and technical skills, the foundation has prioritized programs that bridge the gap between underserved communities and access to technology.

In a rapidly evolving world, the ability to navigate technology is no longer optional; it is essential. TMF organizes training sessions on digital literacy, cybersecurity basics, and job readiness to prepare individuals for the demands of the modern workforce. By focusing on practical, industry-relevant skills, these programs open doors to careers that were once out of reach.

The foundation's focus on technology aligns seamlessly with my professional work in cybersecurity. Advocacy for digital security has been a consistent part of my journey, whether through raising awareness about online threats or providing tools to help individuals protect their digital assets. Cybersecurity is not just a technical field—it is a critical component of modern life, and ensuring its accessibility to diverse populations is a mission I hold close to my heart.

Beyond individual empowerment, TMF is deeply invested in community upliftment. Initiatives such as orphanage visits, widow empowerment programs, and health outreach events reflect the foundation's holistic approach to addressing societal challenges.

One of the most impactful programs has been the widow empowerment initiative, which provides financial aid and vocational training to women who have lost their spouses. This program not only restores dignity and independence to its participants but also strengthens their ability to provide for their families.

The foundation's work also includes organizing community events that reward excellence and inspire ambition. By celebrating achievements and encouraging healthy competition, these events foster a culture of aspiration and resilience.

While my philanthropic work is deeply fulfilling, balancing it with a demanding career in cybersecurity has required intentional effort. As a family man, I understand the importance of maintaining priorities and ensuring that professional or philanthropic responsibilities never overshadow personal commitments.

This balance has shaped my perspective on leadership. True leadership is not about doing everything; it is about doing the right things with focus and integrity. It is about making decisions that reflect both long-term vision and immediate impact, whether in the boardroom, at home, or in the community.

My journey has also reinforced the importance of authenticity in leadership. Building trust, honoring commitments, and staying grounded in values are not just ethical choices—they are the foundation of meaningful influence.

Looking ahead, my focus remains on advancing the foundation's mission and my professional contributions to cybersecurity. The projects currently in development aim to introduce new technologies and methodologies that will enhance digital security on a global scale.

At TMF, the future involves expanding programs to reach even more communities. Plans include launching a global initiative to provide technical training to underserved populations, scaling the scholarship program, and building partnerships with organizations that share our vision of inclusive empowerment.

A belief in the transformative power of innovation drives these efforts. Whether through technology, education, or philanthropy, the goal is to create systems and opportunities that enable individuals and communities to thrive.

These principles of innovation and empowerment aren't limited to TMF's initiatives alone. They extend into every project I've created, each designed to address specific challenges and provide practical solutions for individuals striving to achieve their goals. Two standout examples of this commitment are **VeriPass** and **Credit Veto**—platforms that exemplify the intersection of purpose-driven innovation and practical impact.

Empowering Global Talents Through VeriPass

Opportunities don't always knock loudly; sometimes, they're locked behind complex systems that seem impossible to navigate. For African and Nigerian professionals looking to expand their horizons, the process of securing U.S. visas can feel like a labyrinth.

VeriPass was created to clarify that journey, offering more than just guidance—it provides a tailored strategy to transform potential into progress.

At its core, VeriPass is about positioning talent where it belongs: on a global stage. It's not limited to visa application assistance but extends to building a professional identity. Whether through crafting compelling resumes, creating personalized websites, or securing media features, every element is designed to highlight individual brilliance and ensure visibility in competitive spaces.

This initiative is deeply personal. I've walked paths where resources were scarce and obstacles were abundant. I know the weight of feeling talented yet unseen, of having goals that stretch beyond borders but lack the means to realize them. VeriPass effectively addresses this gap, combining expertise with empathy to ensure no effort is wasted and no potential overlooked.

What sets VeriPass apart is its comprehensive approach. It's not about one-size-fits-all solutions but about recognizing the unique value every client brings. For entrepreneurs, this might mean help setting up U.S.-based companies and establishing professional credibility. For creatives, it could involve publishing books or securing recommendation letters from industry leaders. For professionals, it's about strategically showcasing expertise in ways that resonate with immigration processes and beyond.

Every success story fuels this work. Each approval isn't just a milestone for the individual—it's a ripple effect that influences families, industries, and even economies. VeriPass is a reminder that talent doesn't have to be constrained by borders, and opportunities aren't reserved for the privileged few. As I see it, this is the heart of building a legacy: creating systems that outlast us and continue to empower others.

Empowering Financial Futures with Credit Veto

In my mission to create meaningful change, I recognized that financial health is a cornerstone of personal empowerment. This understanding led to the development of Credit Veto, an AI-driven platform designed to simplify credit repair and management.

Credit Veto offers a streamlined approach to identifying and disputing inaccuracies in credit reports. Leveraging advanced AI technology automates the generation of personalized dispute letters, which are then notarized and sent to credit bureaus on behalf of users. This process saves time and enhances the effectiveness of credit repair efforts.

Beyond dispute resolution, Credit Veto provides users with comprehensive insights into their credit profiles. It offers real-time alerts, monthly scores from all three major credit bureaus, and personalized strategies to improve credit health. This holistic approach empowers individuals to take control of their financial futures confidently.

By integrating Credit Veto into my suite of initiatives, I aim to address the financial challenges that often hinder personal and professional growth. It's about providing accessible tools that enable individuals to overcome obstacles and achieve their goals, reinforcing the broader mission of creating a lasting legacy of impact.

As this book comes to a close, I want to leave you with a challenge: think about the legacy you want to leave. Success is not measured by the accolades you earn or the wealth you accumulate—it is measured by the lives you touch and the change you inspire.

Through the Tolu Michael Foundation and my professional endeavors, I have learned that giving back is not just an act of generosity but a way of life. It is a mindset that turns every success into an opportunity to uplift others and every challenge into a chance to learn and grow.

True leadership is about service, and true impact is about collective progress. I hope that the stories, lessons, and principles shared in this book inspire you to embrace your journey of success and use it as a platform for making a difference.

Together, we can create a world where success is not a privilege but a shared possibility and where every achievement contributes to a legacy of hope, empowerment, and transformation. Let us move forward with purpose, knowing that the greatest impact we can make is the one that endures beyond ourselves.

A Legacy of Impact

At its heart, the Tolu Michael Foundation is more than just an organization—it is my way of ensuring that the lessons I have learned and the opportunities I have been given continue to create ripple effects long after I am gone. The foundation embodies the central message of this book: that success is not just about personal gain but about using what you have achieved to empower others.

Through TMF, I have sought to formalize the values of resilience, discipline, and service that have defined my journey. The scholarships, mentorship programs, and community initiatives are not just acts of philanthropy but investments in a shared future. Every scholarship awarded, every training session conducted, and every life touched contribute to a legacy of empowerment that grows stronger with each passing year.

The foundation is my way of demonstrating that impact does not happen in isolation. Just as my mentors and supporters played pivotal roles in shaping my journey, I am committed to being that same catalyst for others. TMF is a living testament to the idea that leadership is about creating opportunities for others to succeed and ensuring that the cycle of empowerment never ends.

This commitment to creating a legacy ties directly to the overarching theme of this book: success becomes truly meaningful when it extends beyond yourself. Each chapter has explored the strategies and principles that drive progress, but the final measure of success is the ability to leave a lasting imprint on the lives of others. TMF reflects that principle, serving as both a culmination of my experiences and a starting point for countless others to begin their own journeys toward impact and fulfillment.

Conclusion

This book began with a promise: to guide you through the principles, strategies, and real-world insights necessary to accelerate your success and create a lasting impact. As we arrive at the final pages, it's worth revisiting the journey we've taken together, reflecting on the key lessons explored, and laying out a clear path forward to apply these lessons in your life.

From the very beginning, we established the foundation of this journey: the belief that success is not accidental. It is intentional deliberate, and the result of aligning your actions with a clear vision of your goals. Through stories and strategies, we explored how to navigate challenges, leverage opportunities, and build the resilience required to stay the course when obstacles arise.

We started by addressing the importance of clarity in direction. Success begins with knowing where you're headed and why it matters. This means cultivating a mindset that values data-driven decisions, disciplined focus, and the ability to filter out distractions. These principles formed the backbone of the early chapters, where we laid out the significance of refining your vision and creating a strategy to achieve it.

But no vision, no matter how powerful, is immune to the challenges of reality. We discussed the inevitable obstacles—financial struggles, cultural adjustments, fear of failure—and examined how to face them head-on. Whether it was through personal anecdotes or the inspiring stories of others, the message was clear: setbacks are not the end. They are the stepping stones to growth, resilience, and eventual success.

In this book, we also celebrated the transformative power of networks. We discussed how surrounding yourself with the right people can amplify your efforts and open doors to opportunities you might never find alone. Building strategic relationships is not just about who you know—it's about how you engage, contribute, and grow alongside others.

Execution, too, played a central role in our exploration. We examined the art of turning plans into action, emphasizing the importance of prioritization, focus, and disciplined effort. Whether through practical techniques like time-blocking or strategies for balancing speed and precision, the goal was to show you how to bridge the gap between ambition and results.

As we moved forward, the role of technology and innovation took center stage. In today's world, tools like AI, automation, and tailored platforms like ExcelMind and Lightforth are not optional—they are essential. These chapters demonstrated how to harness these resources to accelerate your journey, offering insights into how they can transform not just your career but your approach to problem-solving and execution.

Perhaps most importantly, this book has been about people. From sharing the real-world stories of those who have overcome challenges and achieved success through the principles outlined here to exploring how the Tolu Michael Foundation uplifts communities, the message has been consistent: success is not just about personal gain. It is about creating a ripple effect of impact that benefits others and leaves a legacy of progress and hope.

What's your next step?

The strategies, stories, and insights shared in this book are not meant to sit idle. They are a call to action—a challenge for you to take what you've learned and put it into practice. Whether you're just beginning your journey or looking to take your success to the next level, now is the time to act.

If you've been inspired by the stories of transformation or the strategies outlined here, I encourage you to consider joining the ExcelMindCyber program. This program is designed to provide you with the tools, guidance, and community support you need to break into cybersecurity—a growing and thriving field. With no technical background required, it offers a clear, step-by-step pathway to building a career that aligns with your goals and aspirations.

The program is more than just training. It's a proven system that has helped countless individuals realize their dreams. From personalized resume support to interview preparation and access to a network of industry professionals, ExcelMind equips you with everything you need to succeed.

Imagine where you could be in six months or a year. Imagine the opportunities waiting on the other side of a single decision to invest in yourself. That decision could be the first step toward financial stability, professional growth, and personal fulfillment.

As you close this book, take a moment to reflect on the legacy you want to leave behind. Success, as we've explored, is not just about what you achieve for yourself but about your impact on others. Whether through your career, community, or personal life, every step you take toward growth creates opportunities for those around you.

The lessons in this book are universal, but they are also deeply personal. How you apply them will depend on your unique journey, your aspirations, and your values. My hope is that you leave these pages not just inspired but equipped—with a clear vision, actionable strategies, and the confidence to pursue your goals with determination and purpose.

Leadership is about service, and success is about legacy. As you move forward, remember that every choice you make is an opportunity to contribute to a larger story—one of progress, empowerment, and transformation.

The world needs leaders willing to step up, take risks, and make a difference. Let your journey be a testament to what is possible, and let your legacy be one that inspires others to do the same. The tools are in your hands. The decision is yours to make.

Let's build something extraordinary together.

www.ingramcontent.com/pod-product-compliance
Lightning Source LLC
LaVergne TN
LVHW022222200926
848481LV00006B/2081
* 9 7 9 8 3 4 8 5 1 7 3 6 6 *